TWENTY-ONE WELSH PRINCES
the rulers and ruling families
of medieval Wales

WALIHIS

By the same author:

The Welsh Princes 1063–1283

autoThe Lord Rhys, Prince of Deheubarth

Llywelyn the Great

*Edward VI and Mary I, 1540–58:
a mid-Tudor crisis?*

Henry VII (with Caroline Rogers)

*Henry VIII to Mary:
government and religion 1509–1558*

The Treason and Trial of Sir John Perrot

Histories of Wales: Pembrokeshire

Twenty-one Welsh Princes

the rulers and ruling families
of medieval Wales

Roger Turvey

First published in 2010

© Roger Turvey

© Gwasg Carreg Gwalch 2010

Published with the financial support
of the Welsh Books Council

ISBN: 978-1-84527-269-2

Cover design: Sion Ilar/CLlC.

Published by Gwasg Carreg Gwalch,
12 Iard yr Orsaf, Llanrwst, Wales LL26 0EH
tel: 01492 624031
fax: 01492 641502
email: books@carreg-gwalch.com
internet: www.carreg-gwalch.com

Contents

Introduction

The Welsh Princes

Who and what were the Welsh princes? Put simply, they were men and women of status and power. In a rigidly hierarchical society where status was important, theirs was the most important of all, for by birth, lineage and blood they were royal. Their power too was derived in large part from their royal status, but was dependent also, as befitted a warrior caste, on their courage in combat and leadership on the battlefield. Heroic in deed, dynastic in ambition and rulers by design, the princes were the elite of a privileged aristocratic class. Yet in spite of these shared characteristics it is difficult to categorise the Welsh princes as a group, for although they were royal and they were rulers they were not necessarily equal. Most were rulers of a single kingdom some, by dint of conquest, more than one – but the exceptional among them were able to extend their power over the greater part of Wales. However, such successes could usually be measured in the space of a generation since the gains made by one ruler were, more often than not, lost by another.

Land, lordship and local acknowledgement were among the key determinants of a ruler's status, but war was his badge of honour. The native rulers were a warrior elite. Whereas the majority of their subjects' social and political horizon was bounded by the structures of local life – the village, its church and the lord – the rulers took a broader view of the world that involved kingships and kingdoms. By a process of expansion, definition and development, particularly in the agencies of coercive authority, they, like the rest of Western Europe, worked towards creating coherent territorial principalities. The more successful rulers were those who most effectively wielded power, not just over the peasant element of the population, but over the noble element also. By endeavouring to create an administrative infrastructure for their respective kingdoms, they were attempting to make real and tangible their power and authority. The exceptional among them succeeded in broadening their power by exercising a form of authority over the other native rulers of Wales.

Before 1063 only three native rulers had been able to extend their power over a substantial part of Wales: Rhodri Mawr (d. 878) and Gruffudd ap Llywelyn (d. 1063/4) of Gwynedd, and Hywel Dda (d. 950). Whether any of them had a sense of unity, or were merely war-leaders seeking domination, is open to debate.

After 1063 only two rulers succeeded in extending their hegemony over the greater part of Wales: Llywelyn ap Iorwerth (c.1194–1240) and his grandson Llywelyn ap Gruffudd (1247–82). The key to the success of the two Llywelyns, besides their military muscle, was in bringing to heel the other native rulers within a political framework that tolerated but excluded the Marcher lords, whilst simultaneously seeking acknowledgement of the English Crown of their status.

The Welsh Kingdoms

Wales was a land of many kingdoms and many dynasties, the principal divisions of which, at least by the middle of the eleventh century, were the four major territories of Gwynedd, Powys, Deheubarth and Morgannwg. Unlike Gwynedd and Powys, which had a history stretching back to the departure of the Romans, Morgannwg and Deheubarth were relatively new creations dating to the eighth and tenth centuries respectively. Only three of these kingdoms survived into the twelfth century (Morgannwg falling by the wayside late in the eleventh), of which Gwynedd alone emerged enlarged and strong enough to dominate the Welsh political landscape in the thirteenth.

There had, in the past, been various lesser kingdoms, principal among them Brycheiniog, Dyfed, Gwent and Gwynllwg, but most of these had gradually been absorbed by their more powerful neighbours or, more likely after 1066, had succumbed to conquest by the invading Normans. Remarkably and exceptionally, the minor royal dynasties of Maelienydd, Gwrtheyrnion and Elfael, together making up the region known as Rhwng Gwy a Hafren (literally between the rivers Wye and Severn), largely survived absorption by their Welsh neighbours in the twelfth century, only to be conquered by the English in the thirteenth. The minor rulers of Arwystli and Meirionnydd too enjoyed brief periods of independence when they either resisted, or temporarily strayed from, the control of their respective parent kingdoms of Powys (by annexation) and Gwynedd.

For much of the Middle Ages, the rulers of these various kingdoms were selfishly engaged in their own almost endless political and military competition. Rulers and kingdoms vied with each other for supremacy, thus did successive rulers of Gwynedd make war on their native contemporaries, the rulers of Deheubarth and Powys. Therefore, Wales was manufactured by war and fashioned by the ambitions of a ruler bent on uniting under his command, the territories of his Welsh neighbours whom he sought to make his vassals. Nor was this competition confined to rivalry between kingdoms but involved dynastic struggles within kingdoms also: between 949 and 1066 no fewer than thirty-five rulers were butchered at the hands of their families, friends and compatriots. Membership of the dynasties of Deheubarth and Powys seemed to be among the most precarious, with some fourteen of their number suffering death or maiming at the hands of their dynastic rivals between 1076 and 1160. Only when there emerged a leader of exceptional authority and skill could a kingdom transcend this internal violence and make its mark on the wider political stage.

Gwynedd

The credit for establishing Gwynedd's primacy in Welsh affairs is due, primarily, to the work of two early rulers, Gruffudd ap Cynan (c.1075–1137) and his son Owain ap Gruffudd or, as he is most commonly known, Owain Gwynedd (1137–70). They withstood the external pressures of Marcher ambition and royal intervention whilst repairing the dynastic fissures within that regularly threatened to tear their territorial power apart. Between them, they created a stable and prosperous kingdom by strengthening their hold on church and state and by wisely acknowledging English control. They were also responsible for originating and promoting the idea that a ruler of Gwynedd possessed authority over Wales as a whole, and, as if to emphasise the fact of their primacy, to Owain Gwynedd goes the credit of being among the first of his countrymen to cultivate a diplomatic friendship with a foreign ruler, Louis VII of France (1137–80).

Deheubarth

The composite kingdom of Deheubarth, formed by the enforced merger of three lesser kingdoms, Ceredigion, Dyfed and Ystrad Tywi, had its share of talented rulers during this period, namely, Rhys ap Tewdwr (c.1081–93) and his grandson Rhys ap Gruffudd, popularly known as the Lord Rhys (1155–97). Between them they kept alive a polity which might otherwise have disintegrated long before it actually did so in the early thirteenth century. By sheer force of personality they held together a kingdom that had been manufactured by military might and political will but which was subject to almost overwhelming pressures as much from within as from without. Deheubarth was crushed and dismembered by the Anglo-Normans after the killing of Rhys ap Tewdwr, and it was left to the Lord Rhys to resurrect the kingdom in the second half of the twelfth century, only for it to implode after his death amid a complex tangle of domestic squabbles. Thereafter, its territorially-embarrassed princelings – Maelgwn ap Rhys (d. 1231), Rhys Gryg (d. 1233) and Rhys ap Maredudd (d. 1292) principal among them – became subject either to the rulers of Gwynedd or England depending on the prevailing political situation.

Powys

Geographically locked between the native kingdoms of Gwynedd and Deheubarth on the one side and the alien Marcher lordships on the other, Powys was surrounded by hostile powers willing and eager to seize on any moment of weakness. Its rulers had the unenviable task of maintaining a balance of power that required a political skill and dexterity which only the most talented possessed, and in Madog ap Maredudd (c.1132--60) the Powysian dynasty had found its champion. During Madog's twenty-odd year rule, Powys entered a period of prosperity and relative stability which was only shattered on his death with the partition of the kingdom into Powys Wenwynwyn (or southern Powys) and Powys Fadog (or northern Powys). Although gravely weakened as a result of this partition, particularly in the case of Powys Fadog which suffered further dynastic subdivisions in 1236 and 1269, senior segments of the Powysian dynasty continued to play a role in national affairs. Two of the most significant, by reason of their talent and instinct for survival, hailed from Powys Wenwynwyn, namely, Owain Cyfeiliog (1160–97) and his grandson Gruffudd ap Gwenwynwyn (1216–86). Between them, they managed to keep alive the hopes and aspirations of their dynasty, and their success may be measured inasmuch as their principality was the only one to survive the Edwardian conquest.

English Kings and Norman Marcher Lords

On occasion, the balance of power in this fragmented land turned on the intervention of English kings, all of whom were concerned to maintain Welsh recognition of their power without necessarily having to physically enforce it. At no time before the reign of Edward I (1272–1307) did the Crown contemplate the conquest of Wales being content to demonstrate their power visibly by means of spasmodic, if mainly impressive, military expeditions. In all, twenty-one royal expeditions were launched in Wales between 1081 and 1267, some of the more successful being those led by William I (1066–87) in 1081, Henry I (1100–35) in 1114 and 1121, Henry II (1154–1189) in 1157–8, John (1199–1216) in 1211 and Henry III (1216–72) in 1241 and 1245–6.

The Crown's generally fitful interest in Welsh affairs before the mid to late thirteenth century meant that the balance of power in Wales was more often likely to depend on the emergence of outstandingly able or ruthless native and, after 1066, Marcher leaders. The demise of Morgannwg in the 1080s and '90s at the hands of Marcher barons serves to highlight the new and permanent element that was introduced to the history of Wales by the coming of the Normans. While it might be argued that they came to Wales as much allies as enemies, taking advantage of domestic squabbles to side with one dynastic faction against another, they were, above all, conquerors, freebooting barons intent on carving out for themselves territorial enclaves in this region of the Anglo-Welsh frontier or March. The Marchers' free-enterprise and land-grabbing expeditions along coasts and river valleys, staking their claim by erecting earth and timber castles as they went, transformed the power structure in Wales. By dint of their conquests, the eastern and southern parts of Wales were occupied by Marcher lordships that ranged in size from great earldoms like Pembroke and Glamorgan to lesser entities like Brecon and Gower. Indeed, great Marcher families like Clare, Braose and Mortimer were no less dynastic in outlook than their native counterparts with whom they contended for control of Wales.

It was not until the last quarter of the thirteenth century that a king emerged, Edward I, with the authority, power and drive necessary to effect the conquest of Wales. King Edward used the English state's superior resources in men, money and technology to gain victories over the Welsh. To provide an element of political continuity, and as a means of underlining what he saw as the finality of the English conquest of the Welsh, Edward I appointed his son and heir 'Prince of Wales'. The bestowal of this title in 1301 on the heir to the Crown of England began a tradition that survives to this day but it was and is regarded by some Welsh people as an act of extreme provocation. Later the bestowing of the same title upon Henry (the future Henry V), the son of Henry IV, in 1399 may have been a contributing factor in inflaming Owain Glyndr's uprising in 1400 and of the proclaiming of Owain as the rightful holder of that title.

The Family Trees

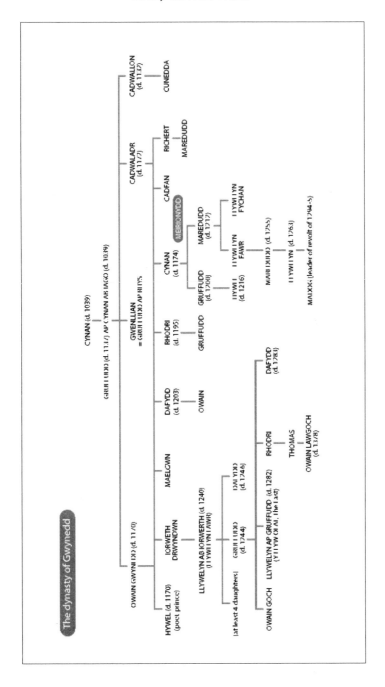

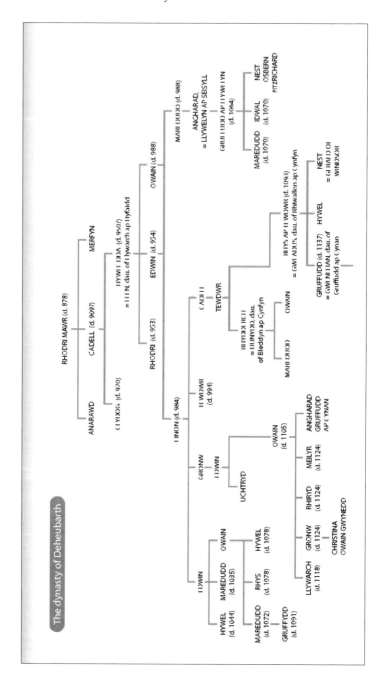

The dynasty of Deheubarth

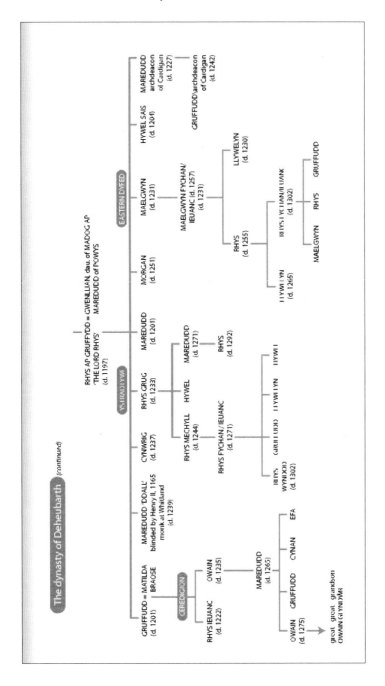

The dynasty of Deheubarth *(continued)*

RHYS AP GRUFFYDD = GWENLLIAN dau. of MADOG AP
'THE LORD RHYS'   MAREDUDD of POWYS
(d. 1197)

The lesser dynasties

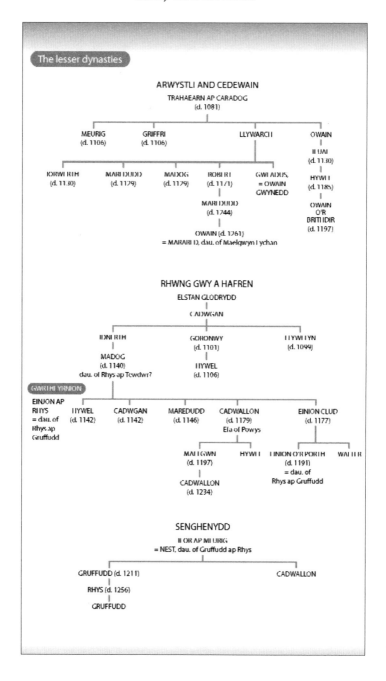

ARWYSTLI AND CEDEWAIN

TRAHAEARN AP CARADOG
(d. 1081)

| MEURIG (d. 1106) | GRIFFRI (d. 1106) | | LLYWARCH | | OWAIN |

OWAIN —
II UAI (d. 1130)

IORWERTH (d. 1130) — MAREDUDD (d. 1129) — MADOG (d. 1129) — ROBERT (d. 1171) — GWLADUS = OWAIN GWYNEDD

HYWEL (d. 1185)

MAREDUDD (d. 1244)

OWAIN O'R BRITHDIR (d. 1197)

OWAIN (d. 1261)
= MARARED, dau. of Maelgwyn Fychan

RHWNG GWY A HAFREN

ELSTAN GLODRYDD

CADWGAN

| IDNERTH | GORONWY (d. 1101) | LLYWELYN (d. 1099) |

MADOG (d. 1140)
dau. of Rhys ap Tewdwr?

HYWEL (d. 1106)

GWRTHEYRNION

EINION AP RHYS = dau. of Rhys ap Gruffudd — HYWEL (d. 1142) — CADWGAN (d. 1142) — MAREDUDD (d. 1146) — CADWALLON (d. 1179) Efa of Powys — EINION CLUD (d. 1177)

MAELGWN (d. 1197) — HYWEL — EINION O'R PORTH (d. 1191) = dau. of Rhys ap Gruffudd — WALTER

CADWALLON (d. 1234)

SENGHENYDD

IFOR AP MEURIG
= NEST, dau. of Gruffudd ap Rhys

| GRUFFUDD (d. 1211) | | CADWALLON |

RHYS (d. 1256)

GRUFFUDD

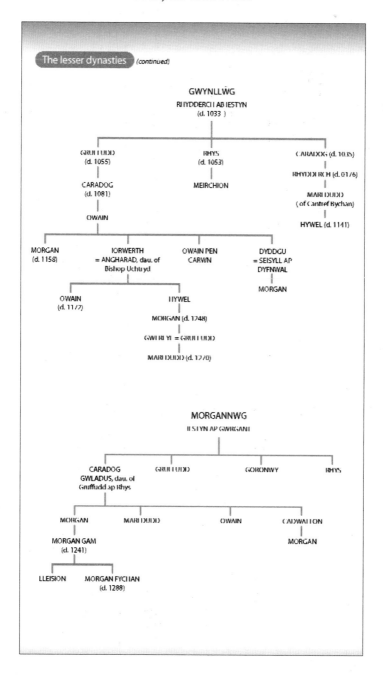

The lesser dynasties *(continued)*

GWYNLLWG

RHYDDERCH AB IESTYN
(d. 1033)

- GRUFFUDD (d. 1055)
  - CARADOG (d. 1081)
    - OWAIN
      - MORGAN (d. 1158)
      - IORWERTH = ANGHARAD, dau. of Bishop Uchtryd
        - OWAIN (d. 1172)
        - HYWEL
          - MORGAN (d. 1248)
            - GWERFYL = GRUFFUDD
              - MAREDUDD (d. 1270)
      - OWAIN PEN CARWN
      - DYDDGU = SEISYLL AP DYFNWAL
        - MORGAN
- RHYS (d. 1053)
  - MEIRCHION
- CARADOG (d. 1035)
  - RHYDDERCH (d. 1076)
    - MAREDUDD (of Cantref Bychan)
      - HYWEL (d. 1141)

MORGANNWG

IESTYN AP GWRGANT

- CARADOG GWLADUS, dau. of Gruffudd ap Rhys
  - MORGAN
    - MORGAN GAM (d. 1241)
      - LLEISION
      - MORGAN FYCHAN (d. 1288)
  - MAREDUDD
  - OWAIN
  - CADWALLON
    - MORGAN
- GRUFFUDD
- GORONWY
- RHYS

17

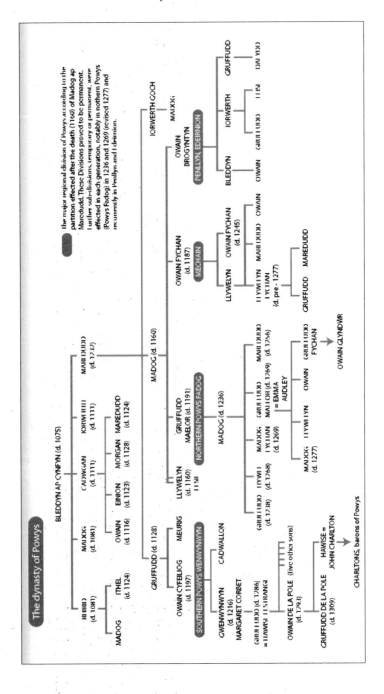

The dynasty of Powys

The major regional division of Powys, according to the partition effected after the death (1160) of Madog ap Maredudd. These Divisions proved to be permanent. Further sub-divisions, temporary or permanent, were effected in each generation, notably in northern Powys (Powys Fadog) in 1236 and 1269 (revised 1277) and recurrently in Penllyn and Edeirnion.

The Biographies

Rhodri Mawr

Rhodri Mawr (d. 878) was the son of Merfyn Frych, king of Gwynedd, and Nest daughter of Cadell ap Brochwel of Powys. At the time of his birth Wales was a land of multiple kingship and kingdoms (see map). Besides fighting each other, the Welsh kingdoms had enemies aplenty outside Wales, most notably the Vikings or Norsemen (from Scandinavia) and the Mercians (an English kingdom in the Midlands). The ninth century has been described as the first Viking Age because it was a period marked by frequent raids and some settlements in and around the British mainland. Place-names such as Anglesey, Skomer, Skokholm, Flat Holm and Swansea (Sweyn's eye) bear witness to the Viking activity around the coasts of Wales.

The first recorded Viking attack on Wales was in 850, but given the level of Viking activity in the Irish Sea from the early part of the century, it is unlikely to represent the first contact between the two peoples. The other threat to Wales came from the Mercians, who pursued an aggressive policy towards the Welsh particularly under the leadership of King Cenwulf. Located in the heart of England, the Midland kingdom of Mercia was well placed to strike anywhere in Wales, and the Mercians did so regularly and with ruthlessness during the ninth century. It was in this climate of fear and tension that the burden and responsibility of kingship was thrust upon Rhodri, who succeeded a father killed in battle.

Rhodri succeeded to the kingdom of Gwynedd in 844 on the death of his father, Merfyn Frych. In spite of his importance, as implied by the epithet Great, very little is known about his deeds within Wales, and most of what we do know has come down to us from later accounts. More is known of his dealings with the Saxon-English and Scandinavian-Vikings, from which contact it can be surmised that he was a capable ruler and a good soldier. Rhodri early showed signs of his ability and ambition, the primary focus of which was the securing of his power in Gwynedd. It is likely that he achieved this by being ruthless and through the indiscriminate use of violence, but the details of his rise to power elude us.

Having secured his position in Gwynedd Rhodri turned to defending his kingdom from the predatory raids of both Vikings and Saxons. This he managed successfully until 853 when the military forces of Burgred of Mercia and Æthelwulf of Wessex combined to invade Wales. Their success was such that a number of Welsh rulers offered their submissions to the victorious Saxon kings. A reluctant Rhodri is thought to have been among them.

Undeterred by this military setback, and doubtless respecting the limits imposed by Burgred and Æthelwulf to Welsh expansionism eastward towards England, Rhodri set about expanding his authority within Wales. In 855 Rhodri acquired control of neighbouring Powys when its ruler, Cyngen ap Cadell, died in Rome.

Why Cyngen ventured so far from home is not known but it is thought that he might have died on pilgrimage to the Holy City. If this is the case then he would have been the first Welsh ruler to be recorded as doing so and, more significantly, among the first to indicate a willingness to recognise the authority of the papacy over the Celtic Church in Wales.

Having been isolated from the Roman Church for some centuries on account of the Saxon conquest of England, the Celtic Church had developed customs and practices that were different and unique to Wales. Among the more important was the right to the hereditary succession of Church property and marriage of the clergy. However, as Saxon England converted to the Christian faith during the seventh century the isolation of the Celtic Church diminished, and over a 200-year period, roughly between the early eighth and mid ninth centuries, its constituent parts in Ireland, southern Scotland, Cornwall and Wales, gradually accepted the authority of Rome.

Rhodri's relationship with and his attitude to the Church is not known but his uncle's death presented him with an opportunity for expansion that he was quick to seize. He is thought to have annexed Powys on account of being the son of Cyngen's sister Nest, and the fact that Cyngen is known to have had sons seems not to have deterred Rhodri who took control of the kingdom in defiance of royal rules of inheritance.

Within months of celebrating his success in acquiring Powys he faced the full force of a Viking raid on Anglesey. Known as the Black Host (or *Dub Gaill*), this group of Vikings had long been settled in Dublin and their control of the Irish Sea proved to be a formidable threat to the Welsh. The outcome of the raid on Anglesey is unknown but its success may be gauged by the fact that less than a year later, in 856, they returned. Led by Gorm, a Viking chief of fearsome reputation, the raiders did not bargain on Rhodri's stout defence of the island, and in a hard-fought battle Gorm was killed. The site of the encounter is not known but Rhodri's victory over the Vikings may be that celebrated in the poem by Sedulius Scottus, an Irishman working on the continent.

Having seen off the Vikings, Rhodri was next attacked by the Saxons who drove him from Anglesey in 865. He returned shortly after to wreak his revenge and wrest control of the island from the enemy. In 872 fate intervened to present Rhodri with an opportunity to annex the agriculturally-rich kingdom of Ceredigion when its last king, Gwgon ap Meurig (the brother of Rhodri's wife Angharad), met his death through drowning. Whether this was by accident or by design is not known, but given Rhodri's ambition and propensity for violence his hand in the affair cannot be ruled out.

Within Wales Rhodri's expansionist policies had met with unprecedented success, but in order to maintain his control of what, in effect, was a loose confederation of at least three Welsh kingdoms – Gwynedd, Powys and Ceredigion – he had to defend himself from both Saxons and Vikings who viewed his rise to power with alarm.

Due in the main to military pressure exerted by the Mercians and Vikings of Dublin, the last years of Rhodri's reign witnessed a number of encounters that were not successful for him. In 877 the Vikings succeeded in defeating Rhodri in battle and driving him into exile in southern Ireland. He was back within a year but was slain, alongside his son Gwriad, by the Mercians led by Æthelred in 878.

Rhodri is credited with having a number of sons, and of these

Anarawd and Cadell are the most notable in seeking to continue their father's expansionist policy. Rhodri may never have ruled all of Wales, but the fact that a majority of Welsh rulers in the tenth and later centuries claimed descent from him is perhaps indicative of his contemporary political reputation and later genealogical importance.

The reign of Rhodri Mawr has been described as a turning point in the history of Wales, because it witnessed for the first time a temporary association of powerful Welsh kingdoms that gave rise to thoughts of political and territorial unity.

Hywel Dda

Hywel (d. 949/50) was the son of Cadell and the grandson of Rhodri Mawr. His impeccable royal pedigree ensured that he would be a contender for power when he grew to manhood. Whether he achieved power, of course, depended as much as on his own skill and daring as on fate – and perhaps a little luck.

Hywel occupies a special place in the history of Wales, being the only Welsh king to have been called 'the Good' – presumably on account of his effective rule and reputation for law-making. Indeed, it has been suggested that after his death Hywel became the centre of a cult that held him to be the ideal of early medieval kingship – pious, just and soldierly. On the other hand, it has also been suggested that he may have been responsible for the murder of his wife's uncle, an act that, if ever it could be proved, would somewhat tarnish his reputation for doing 'good'.

The first half of the tenth century was a relatively peaceful period for Wales. The frequency and seriousness of Viking raids had decreased and the rulers of the kingdoms of Mercia and Wessex were more concerned with re-conquering those parts of England settled by the Vikings than with conflict with the Welsh. Thus, Hywel and his brother Clydog succeeded to the rulership of Seisyllwg, a kingdom consisting of Ceredigion and Ystrad Tywi at a time of peace. Here they ruled jointly from 903 until Clydog's death in 920 when Hywel became sole ruler. Freed from the constraints imposed by partnership, Hywel thrived, and by the time of his death, in 949 or 950, his rule extended to over three quarters of Wales.

The gradual extension of Hywel's power over most of Wales, with the exception of the kingdoms of the south-east, was achieved through a combination of marriage alliances, political opportunism and war. His first acquisition was the kingdom of Dyfed (roughly equivalent with modern Pembrokeshire) which he added to his territorial portfolio through marriage with Elen, the daughter and heiress of Llywarch ap Hyfaidd.

The death of Llywarch in 903, and the murder, by decapitation, of his brother Rhodri in 904, for which Hywel might have been responsible, cleared the way for the annexation of Dyfed and the creation of the composite kingdom of Deheubarth. Dynastic rivalry was a fact of life for an ambitious Welsh ruler and it is perhaps no surprise to learn that Hywel too was subject to the machinations of others. Hywel's successful partnership with his brother Clydog came to a bloody end when the latter was slain by a third brother Meurig. Meurig, along with a half-brother Gwriad and Clydog's son Hyfaidd, proved troublesome and they remained a threat to Hywel until at least 938.

Hywel did not let these domestic distractions hinder his wider ambitions, the most important of which was the maintenance of peace with the English kings. Recognising the growing power of Wessex, Hywel was keen to cultivate the friendship of its king Edward the Elder, a warrior with a fine military reputation. In 918 Hywel offered his submission, along with Clydog and Idwal Foel of Gwynedd, to Edward at Tamworth.

However, it is with Edward's son and heir Æthelstan that Hywel is most frequently linked.

In 926 Æthelstan received the submission of all the kings in Wales at Hereford, where he is said to have exacted an annual tribute from them. For the remainder of his reign Hywel regularly attended this English king and later his brother Eadred, meeting them on no fewer than ten occasions between 928 and 949. Hywel's relationship with, and frequent visits to, England need not suggest a man subservient to the will of the English. On the contrary, it suggests that he was astute enough to recognize the superior power of English kings such as Æthelstan, and that his visits were made more out of political expediency than out of admiration for a more powerful neighbour. Indeed, Hywel's apparent compliance with English authority enabled him to pursue his territorial ambitions in Wales unhindered, free from the threat of English intervention.

In 942 Hywel more than doubled his territorial power in Wales when, on the death of Idwal Foel, king of Gwynedd, he invaded and conquered the northern kingdom. Hywel's annexation of Gwynedd was challenged by Idwal's sons, Iago and Ieuaf, but they were defeated and forced into exile. Hywel's growing power was recognised by the English who referred to him in charters thereafter as *rex* or *regulus* (king) rather than the *subregulus* (sub-king) of old.

Hywel, too, may have begun to appreciate the political benefits of cultivating his image as a king of wide authority and outstanding ability, being the only early medieval Welsh ruler to have issued coinage. The single example of his silver penny bearing the legend 'Howæl Rex' was a product of his close relationship with the English, who appear to have permitted his use of the mint at Chester.

Perhaps the innovation for which Hywel is most famous for is the codification and promulgation of Welsh customary law. Although the earliest surviving copies of the native law books can only be dated to the late twelfth and early thirteenth century, some 300 years after Hywel's death, the preface to each law book acknowledges a debt to the work of Hywel ap Cadell, 'prince of all Wales'.

Hywel is said to have convened an assembly of men, mainly ecclesiastics, six of whom were to be drawn from every hundred, a district comprising a hundred villages, from across Wales at Whitland. After some forty days of deliberation the laws were amended and redacted, and were known consequently as *Cyfraith Hywel* ('the law of Hywel')

One remarkable feature of these laws is their recognition of the legal status of women. Whereas in the rest of western Europe women were regarded merely as the property of their menfolk, a status that persisted for centuries, in Wales they had the right to divorce and to reclaim the property that they had brought into the marriage.

As one might expect, instances of crime and punishment feature prominently in the law books. For example, there was no capital punishment for murder: the perpetrator's family had to pay a *galanas* or murder price to the family of the deceased; but a thief caught stealing property could be hanged. On the other hand, a person apprehended for stealing food might be pardoned if he could prove that he had been begging in vain for three days in an attempt to feed his starving family. Careful study of the laws show that they were comprehensive, sophisticated and sufficient for almost every occasion.

Although Hywel's law-making is likely based in fact, the extent of his achievement has perhaps been exaggerated by later rulers like the twelfth-century prince of Deheubarth, the Lord Rhys. In common with other rulers of his time, Rhys ap Gruffudd was keen to revise and control the Welsh laws as a means of strengthening his own power. One of the methods employed by Rhys to gain acceptance for these laws was to suggest an ancient provenance by linking them to a name rooted in antiquity; Hywel Dda seemed to fit the bill. Indeed, it is a fact that Hywel's epithet 'the good' does not predate the twelfth century.

Nevertheless, to dismiss Hywel's responsibility for law-making would be a mistake. He was clearly a man of vision and wide experience, as his visit on pilgrimage to Rome in 929 indicates. Whether or not this excursion, made after the death of his wife, deserves to be described, in the words of Stephen Williams as 'one of the outstanding incidents in his life', there is no doubt that he was an outstanding ruler whose enlarged kingdom could not, and did not, long survive his death.

Gruffudd ap Llywelyn

Gruffudd ap Llywelyn (d. 1063) was king of Gwynedd from 1039 to 1063 and of Deheubarth from 1055 until his death. In terms of his royal blood and lineage, all Gruffudd had to recommend him was his claim to descend from Hywel Dda through his mother Angharad. Indeed, Gruffudd's own parentage is rather obscure and difficult to trace. His father, Llywelyn ap Seisyll, cannot be linked with any known lineage, and although later genealogies suggest that his mother (Gruffudd's grandmother) was a descendant of Rhodri Mawr of Gwynedd, this claim is unproven.

Gruffudd's claim to rule Gwynedd came via his father, a powerful local nobleman who either had to be won over or subdued by those seeking to rule the kingdom. In the event, it was Llywelyn who defeated his enemies and ruled Gwynedd from 1018 until his death in 1023. However, Llywelyn's usurpation meant that his son's succession would likely be challenged, and this is what happened when Iago ab Idwal seized the throne and re-established the old line of Gwynedd.

Gruffudd's whereabouts at this time are unknown but he may have fled to the relative safety of Ireland. The only evidence we have of his youth comes from the writings of Walter Map, a Welsh cleric from Herefordshire who wrote his book *De Nugis Curialium (Trifles of Courtiers)*, sometime in the 1180s. Map presented Gruffudd as a spineless youth, lacking in confidence and ambition, and as someone unlikely ever to rule a kingdom. Urged on by his sister Gruffudd apparently changed his ways and in 1039 he engineered a coup in Gwynedd that led to the overthrow and murder of its king, Iago.

Gruffudd proved to be an aggressive and powerful ruler of Gwynedd whose ruthlessness was to strike fear into the hearts of his enemies. Soon after securing Gwynedd, Gruffudd found himself in conflict with the Mercians, whom he defeated at Rhyd-y-groes on the Severn. Gruffudd's victory impressed itself on the English, who were deterred from attacking him again. Having secured his frontier from attack by the English, Gruffudd concentrated on making himself ruler of Deheubarth.

The conquest of Deheubarth proved to be a difficult proposition. He was opposed by Hywel ab Edwin and Gruffudd ap Rhydderch who between them managed to prevent Gruffudd achieving his ambition until the latter's death in 1055. Twice, in 1039 and 1041, Gruffudd defeated Hywel and even captured his wife, but he failed to take his kingdom. Such were the fortunes of war that within months of returning to Gwynedd from the south Gruffudd was captured by a Scandinavian force in 1042.

How Gruffudd obtained his freedom is not known but the episode convinced Hywel that an alliance with the Scandinavians was worth having. In the event the alliance achieved little for Gruffudd defeated them and killed Hywel in 1044. However, he could not prevent Gruffudd ap Rhydderch from establishing himself as king of Deheubarth in Hywel's place. Consequently, there was heavy fighting between them in 1045 but neither side could secure ultimate victory.

To tip the balance his way, in 1046 Gruffudd ap Llywelyn allied with an English earl, Swein son of Godwine, and they campaigned together in Wales. The campaign proved a disaster for Gruffudd when the men of Ystrad Tywi attacked his bodyguard – his *teulu* – and killed around 140 of them. This seriously weakened Gruffudd, who had to break off hostilities and return north to recover his military strength. The recovery took some years but by 1052 his forces were strong enough to mount a raid on Herefordshire. The death of Gruffudd ap Rhydderch in 1055, and the absence of a strong candidate to replace him, enabled Gruffudd ap Llywelyn to secure control of Deheubarth and thus come to rule the greater part of Wales.

From 1055 to 1063 Gruffudd was primarily concerned with relations with England. He adopted an aggressive policy towards the English by continually probing the frontier for weaknesses. Gruffudd's dominant position in Wales enabled him to interfere in the domestic politics of his more powerful neighbour, and when in 1055 Ælfgar, son of Leofric, earl of Mercia, was forced into exile in the course of a power struggle between the earls of Wessex and Mercia, he found a willing ally in the Welsh king. Together Gruffudd and Ælfgar defeated a powerful army under Ralph de Mantes, earl of Hereford, and they took the town of Hereford and its cathedral, both of which were razed to the ground.

The English king, Edward the Confessor, responded by appointing Harold, earl of Wessex, to command an army in anticipation of bringing Gruffudd to battle. However, Harold was content to refortify Hereford, and to negotiate peace terms. This angered Leofgar, the new bishop of Hereford, and in the summer of 1056, he led an army against Gruffudd, and was soundly defeated, with heavy losses. Despite his military success, Gruffudd was happy to restore the terms of the peace and even to promise that he would be a faithful under-king or *subregulus* to Edward. According to Walter Map the two rulers came face to face on opposite banks of the Severn, each waiting for the other to make the first move. When Edward the Confessor set out from Aust in a small boat, Gruffudd leapt into the river to meet him and carried him on his shoulders to the shore.

The peace proved to be an uneasy one. In 1057 or 1058 Gruffudd's marriage with Ealdgyth, daughter of Earl Ælfgar, alarmed king Edward who realised that the Mercian–Welsh alliance would be strengthened. In the summer of 1062, Ælfgar suddenly died at which point Earl Harold was sent on a surprise attack on Gruffudd's court at Rhuddlan, but the prince escaped by sea. A campaign was mounted against the Welsh in the summer of 1063 led by Earl Harold. The English exerted so much pressure that in August Gruffudd was killed by his enemies in Wales. His head was taken to Earl Harold, and ultimately delivered to Edward the Confessor. Gwynedd and Powys were given to his half-brothers, Bleddyn and Rhiwallon, who ruled as client kings, and in the south the old dynasty of Deheubarth was restored.

Gruffudd's reign was important for Wales. Territorial gains which he had made along the frontier extended Welsh rule eastwards. His alliance with Mercia gave him greater influence in

English affairs than any other Welsh ruler of the eleventh century. The *Brut y Tywysogyon* praised him as 'the head and shield of the Britons', who gave Wales unity for a brief eight years. His death marked the return of Wales to its traditional pattern of multiple kingship and bloody rivalries.

Bleddyn ap Cynfyn

Bleddyn ap Cynfyn (d. 1075) was the son of Cynfyn ap Gwerystan, probably a nobleman from Powys, and Angharad, daughter of Maredudd ab Owain (d. 999), ruler of Deheubarth. Bleddyn's mother was the widow of Llywelyn ap Seisyll and the mother of Gruffudd ap Llywelyn.

As the half-brother of one of the most powerful kings of Wales, Bleddyn was well placed to take advantage of the untimely death of Gruffudd ap Llywelyn in 1063. It is tempting to suggest that he may have been party to the murder of King Gruffudd through the 'treachery of his [Gruffudd's] own men'. Bleddyn certainly had much to gain through the death of his half-brother. Indeed, according to English sources Edward the Confessor granted Bleddyn and his brother Rhiwallon the lands of their half-brother in return for promises of service and tribute. Was this a reward for services rendered? Whatever the truth of the matter Bleddyn succeeded to the kingship of Gwynedd and Powys at a critical time in the history of Wales coming as it did on the cusp of the Norman takeover of England.

From 1063 until 1069 Bleddyn shared the rulership of Gwynedd and Powys with his brother Rhiwallon. Together they repudiated their agreement with Edward the Confessor by launching a devastating attack on English settlements in Archenfield on the Welsh-Herefordshire border. Two years later, in 1067, they joined Eadric the Wild of Mercia in an attack on the Normans in Herefordshire, which they followed up in 1068 with military assistance for earls Edwin and Morcar in their revolt against William I. Bleddyn's successful partnership with Rhiwallon came to an abrupt end only on the latter's death in the battle of Mechain instigated by his half-nephews, Maredudd and Ithel, the sons of Gruffudd ap Llywelyn; they too were slain. Twelve years later in 1081 Rhiwallon's son Meilyr was also killed in battle at Mynydd Carn.

Bleddyn survived the battle to take his place among the most powerful rulers in Wales. This fact combined with his previously aggressive action against King William, led to his becoming a target of Norman aggression in north Wales. According to Orderic Vitalis Bleddyn was ambushed by the ruthless Robert of Rhuddlan in 1073 who 'made him fly abandoning rich booty'. Robert had been handed a licence to ravage and conquer in Wales by a king determined to curb the aggressive and predatory raids of the troublesome Welsh. Bleddyn realised, perhaps too late, that the Norman presence in Wales posed a greater threat to his power than that of his Welsh rivals. Nevertheless, it was his involvement in a Welsh dispute between the rival claimants of Deheubarth that led to his death in 1075. Drawn south in aid of Rhys ab Owain, ruler of Deheubarth, Bleddyn was apparently murdered as a result of the 'the treachery of the evil-spirited rulers and chief men of Ystrad Tywi'. This suggests that he may have been lured south on false promises and there killed by his erstwhile ally Rhys, a man who later proved himself to be a most cunning and dangerous adversary for those who crossed his path.

According to historian Sir John Edward Lloyd, Bleddyn's 'virtues were those of the ideal prince – clemency, kindness, affability, liberality to the weak and defenceless, respect for the rights of the Church'. He is even credited with making some positive amendments to the laws of Hywel Dda, being one of only two Welsh rulers to whom the law books attribute changes to the native law. Of course, we must never forget that he was a ruler capable of taking tough decisions and a soldier willing to be ruthless on the battlefield. Bleddyn was succeeded by his son Maredudd who ruled Powys until his death in 1132.

Rhys ap Tewdwr

Rhys ap Tewdwr (d. 1093) was directly descended from Hywel Dda. He became king of Deheubarth in 1079, after the murder of Rhys ab Owain, his second cousin. Rhys's succession was not guaranteed since he was hard pressed by a rival for the throne in Caradog ap Gruffudd, described by Kari Maund as 'one of the most aggressive kings of the period'. That Rhys succeeded in defeating his enemy and securing the kingdom against the odds speaks volumes for his character and leadership. Rhys's succession coincided with the greater involvement of the Normans in Welsh affairs. The victory at Hastings of Duke William over King Harold in 1066 had yet to fully impress itself on the Welsh, who probably rejoiced at the news of the death of their old adversary.

Unfortunately for the Welsh, the Normans would prove to be every bit as dangerous an adversary as Harold had been, perhaps more so. Their introduction to Wales of the castle (mainly earth and timber motte and bailey castles) and the armoured knight, together with a more formidable fighting ethos, would change the country forever. Rhys ap Tewdwr became the first Welsh ruler to fully comprehend the nature of the threat posed by these new continental enemies. He fought the Normans doggedly and when circumstances allowed he was drawn into an accommodation with their king but the fact that he was later killed by them sets the pattern for the next two hundred years of Welsh history.

For two or three years after his accession in 1079 Rhys was harassed by the attacks of the Vikings from Ireland and by Caradog ap Gruffudd, who had now made himself master of Gwent and Morgannwg. By 1081 Rhys was in need of allies, and when Gruffudd ap Cynan of Gwynedd returned to Wales from exile in Ireland, he landed near St. David's, and the two princes formed an alliance. They then marched together against Caradog ap Gruffudd and his allies Trahaearn ap Caradog and Meilyr ap Rhiwallon, who met them at 'Mynydd Carn', a place yet to be identified, but probably in north Pembrokeshire in the Preseli mountains. There a decisive battle was fought, in which Caradog, Trahaearn, and Meilyr were killed, and the kingships of Gwynedd and Deheubarth were permanently secured to the descendants of Gruffudd and Rhys respectively.

However, the alliance proved rather less permanent and within a short time the two fell out. The cause and outcome of this quarrel is not known, but suffice to say Rhys survived to take his place as the ruler of Deheubarth. Indeed, such was his growing power and influence that the victor of Hastings, King William, came to south Wales in 1081 to meet him. The two met in St. David's cathedral, and an agreement was drawn up whereby Rhys acknowledged William as his overlord in return for recognition of his position and protection from his enemies. According to the Domesday Book, the agreement was ratified by Rhys who agreed to pay the king the sum of £40 per annum.

Rhys ruled the kingdom in relative peace until 1088, when Madog, Cadwgan, and Rhirid, sons of Bleddyn ap Cynfyn of Powys, drove him into exile in Ireland. Before the end of the year, however, he had returned with Irish assistance, and defeated the three in the battle of 'Llech-y-Crau' in which Madog and Rhirid were killed. Another threat to Rhys came in 1091 when he was challenged by Gruffudd ap Maredudd. Gruffudd had lived in exile in England for a number of years but on the death of William in 1087 he made plans to return to Wales.

William's death weakened Rhys, who would not or could not come to a similar agreement with the old king's successor, his son William Rufus. It has been suggested that Rufus may have encouraged Gruffudd ap Maredudd to mount his challenge for the throne of Deheubarth in order to destabilise Rhys. The two came to battle at Llandudoch (St Dogmaels) in 1091 with Rhys emerging the victor. His victory was short-lived, however, when in the Easter week of 1093 Rhys met the new Norman settlers of Brycheiniog in battle, and was slain. Led by Bernard de Neufmarche, the Normans were now beginning to make their presence felt in south Wales and within a few short years of Rhys's death the kingdom of Deheubarth had been destroyed.

The significance of Rhys ap Tewdwr's reign can be gauged by the language used by both John of Worcester, an Anglo-Norman chronicler, and the anonymous author of one version of the Welsh Chronicles, the *Brut y Tywysogyon*, which implied that his death was believed to have put an end to kingship in Wales.

Gruffudd ap Cynan

Gruffudd ap Cynan was half Welsh and half Viking. His father, Cynan, the direct descendant of the kings of Gwynedd, had fled to Dublin and had there married Ragnhildr, daughter of Olaf (Amlaíb) Sihtricson (d. 981), king of Dublin. Five times in the next twenty-five years Gruffudd was to land in Wales from the long low ships and square sails of his mother's people and fight for his father's kingdom, until, by 1100, it was surely his.

At first Gruffudd did not have much success against his rivals for the throne of Gwynedd. In 1081, however, Gruffudd landed at St. David's and joined forces with Rhys ap Tewdwr who was pursuing his claim to the kingship of Deheubarth. Together they won a great victory at the bloody battle of Mynydd Carn in the Preseli hills, Pembrokeshire. Later that same year King William, while on a pilgrimage to St. David's cathedral, accepted Rhys ap Tewdwr's claim to rule Deheubarth but rejected Gruffudd's. Not long after the victory at Mynydd Carn, Gruffudd was tricked by the Normans, captured by Robert of Rhuddlan, and imprisoned in the border city of Chester. Here he languished for some twelve years seemingly bereft of hope.

However, with the aid of a young man from the district known as Edeirnion, Cynwrig Hir, he escaped. According to a near contemporary source, Cynwrig 'took him [Gruffudd] upon his shoulders and bore him away unperceived, and journeyed he and his companions in the afternoon when the burgesses were eating, and maintained him in his own house for a number of days secretly'.

Gruffudd returned to Gwynedd and, with the help of Cadwgan, ruler of Powys, he drove the Normans out of Gwynedd and destroyed their castles. Apart from one short period in 1098–99, Gruffudd held his kingdom for over forty years. His period of wandering and exile was over.

Gruffudd spent the next twenty years securing his power in Gwynedd. He refused to help his son-in-law, Gruffudd ap Rhys ap Tewdwr, in his fight to regain the kingdom of Deheubarth for fear of provoking the Normans into war. He used the peace to strengthen and enrich his kingdom. He ruled firmly, encouraged agriculture, built churches, and patronized music and poetry. According to a later Tudor tradition, it was Gruffudd who first formed the bards of Wales into an order and drew up the rules of their art. Gruffudd's main achievement was in showing his fellow-Welshman what was possible if they stood up against the invading Normans. At his death in 1137, the Welsh chroniclers celebrated his achievement by calling him the 'defender and pacifier of all Wales'.

Gwenllian, daughter of Gruffudd ap Cynan and wife of Gruffudd ap Rhys

Gwenllian (d. 1136) was the daughter of Gruffudd ap Cynan, ruler of Gwynedd, and Angharad, the daughter of Owain ab Edwin of Deheubarth. Little is known of her or the life she led and but for a single reference to her part in a momentous battle she might have died in utter obscurity. However, this was not to be.

> It was in this region (Cydweli), after the death of Henry I, King of the English, and at a moment when her husband, Gruffudd ap Rhys, Prince of South Wales, had gone to North Wales for reinforcements, that Princess Gwenllian rode forward at the head of an army, like some second Penthesilea, Queen of the Amazons.

Thus was she described by one near to her in blood, the Cambro-Norman cleric, scholar, writer and traveller Gerald de Barri or, as he is better known to posterity, Giraldus Cambrensis (Gerald of Wales). Born at Manorbier in Pembrokeshire in 1147, Gerald was a product of the social and cultural diversity of the March, the son of an Anglo-Norman Marcher lord, William de Barri, and his half-Welsh wife, Angharad. The fact that Gerald's mother was a grand-daughter of Rhys ap Tewdwr enabled him to move easily in Welsh and Anglo-Norman society. In addition, the fact that his grandmother Nest was the sister of Gruffudd ap Rhys, the husband of Gwenllian, adds weight to the accuracy and reliability of his statement.

For some reason the Welsh chroniclers opted to ignore Gwenllian's exploits on the battlefield, an omission that may have had something to do with the fact that her expedition proved a disaster. According to Gerald,

> She was beaten in battle by Maurice de Londres, who ruled over the district at that time, and by Geoffrey, the Bishop's constable

(Bishop Roger of Salisbury). She was so sure of victory that she had brought her two sons with her. One of them, called Morgan, was killed, and the other, called Maelgwn, was captured.

Although described by Gerald as 'a simple sort of man', Maurice was 'very jealous of his possessions' and in spite of his great victory Gwenllian was not spared his wrath. Her head was cut off, along with the heads of 'many of her followers'. It is perhaps fortuitous that Gwenllian, the mother of eight, chose only to take her two youngest children – one a babe in arms – with her to the battlefield, for if she had taken her four-year-old son Rhys, later to find fame as the Lord Rhys, the course of Welsh history might have been irrevocably changed for the worse.

Gwenllian's death was soon avenged, for within months her husband Gruffudd, in alliance with her brothers Owain and Cadwaladr, had routed an Anglo-Norman army at the battle of Crug Mawr near Cardigan. The defeat was far more crushing than that inflicted by Maurice on the Welsh under Gwenllian. This fact prompted Gwynfor Evans, former MP and President of Plaid Cymru, to declare that Gwenllian's 'sacrifice' had not been 'in vain'.

The significance of Gwenllian's actions in 1136 should not be underestimated for, as Gwynfor Evans said, 'No women military leaders had been seen for a thousand years, not since the days of Boadicea and Cartimandua'. In his opinion Gwenllian 'is unique in Welsh history, a heroine who died in battle, fighting for her country when it was crushed under the foot of the Norman invader'. The site of the battle is forever enshrined in the name Maes Gwenllian, and there is a memorial to her in the grounds of Cydweli castle.

Famed for her military misadventure, Gwenllian's gift to posterity may not lie entirely in the field of conflict but in the no less daunting arena of cultural patronage. If historian Andrew Breeze is to be believed, and there are many who do not share his opinion, Gwenllian may have been personally responsible for writing some of the eleven medieval Welsh prose tales known collectively as the *Mabinogion*.

Madog ap Maredudd

Madog ap Maredudd (d. 1160), prince of Powys, was the son of Maredudd ap Bleddyn ap Cynfyn (d. 1132). Madog was born into one of the most vicious and competitive royal families in Wales. The dynasty of Powys was distinguished by the sheer cruelty and brutality its members practised on each other. In a particularly bloody period spanning some seven years, between 1125 and 1132, the Welsh Chronicles record the murder, maiming and imprisonment of a host of unfortunates. For example, in 1125 'strife was bred between Morgan and Maredudd, sons of Cadwgan ap Bleddyn, and in that strife Morgan slew with his own hand Maredudd his brother'. Sympathy for Maredudd's plight is tempered somewhat by the realisation that some months earlier he had done nothing to prevent his son Gruffudd from killing 'Ithel ap Rhiddid ap Bleddyn, his first cousin, in the presence of Maredudd his father'. The Chronicles record further instances of brute insensitivity when in 1131 'Llywelyn ab Owain was deprived of his eyes and his testicles by Maredudd ap Bleddyn', to be followed in 1131 by Meurig being 'deprived of his two eyes and his two testicles'.

Although Gerald of Wales admits that the act of blinding and castration was widely practised across Europe, his complaint lay in the fact that in Wales it was done to kith and kin, including children, rather than to the enemy captured in battle. Given the circumstances of his upbringing Madog was perhaps fortunate to succeed his father as sole ruler of Powys on the latter's death in 1132. Unsurprisingly Madog sought to strengthen his position by maintaining close control over the sons of his elder brother, Gruffudd (d. 1128), as well as over his own younger brother, Iorwerth Goch. The medieval Welsh prose tale (one of eleven collectively known as the *Mabinogion*), 'The dream of Rhonabwy', composed in the late thirteenth century, claims that relations between Madog and his brother were particularly strained, perhaps because Iorwerth refused what some might have thought was a generous offer: to serve as his brother's *penteulu* (captain of his retinue). Iorwerth preferred landholding to service, but his brother was not prepared to share or part with any of his patrimony.

Madog was well aware that close supervision of his own family must go hand in hand with keeping a watchful eye on Gwynedd. The ruling dynasty of his nearest neighbour was both ambitious and aggressive, so Madog adopted the twin policy of military preparedness in the event of an attack and diplomatic dialogue in an attempt to forestall an invasion. The latter policy appeared to bear fruit when Madog successfully negotiated a political alliance with Gwynedd by marrying Susanna, the daughter of Gruffudd ap Cynan. This marriage alliance brought seventeen years of peace between Powys and Gwynedd, until that peace was shattered in 1149 when Madog's brother-in-law, Owain Gwynedd, attacked and occupied the commote of Iâl and built a castle at Tomen y Rhodwydd.

Ironically the destruction of Tomen y Rhodwydd and the recapture of Ial was accomplished by Madog's brother Iorwerth Goch, who may have retained the commote and thus satisfied his ambition to acquire a patrimony of his own. This is not to suggest that Madog had no personal territorial ambitions but, with the possible exception of the lordship of Arwystli which he seized from its ruler Hywel ab Ieuaf, his aggressive tendencies were directed, in the main, towards acquiring the rich Anglo-Norman manors of Shropshire. Madog's success in Shropshire, underlined by his siege and capture of the castle of Oswestry and the killing of Stephen fitz Baldwin, constable of Montgomery Castle, owed much to the opportunities created by the weakness of the English crown and Marcher lords in the border counties during the reign of Stephen. The success of Madog's military campaigns against the English in Shropshire were celebrated by the court poets Gwalchmai ap Meilyr and Cynddelw Brydydd Mawr.

Iorwerth's fear of his brother pushed him into the arms of the English who welcomed the opportunity to undermine Madog's position in Powys. Perhaps in an attempt to deter Madog from acquiring more landholdings in Shropshire, Stephen's successor as king of England, Henry II, granted Iorwerth the manor of Sutton near Wenlock in the county. In an effort to better understand the problems confronting him in Wales, it is possible that the newly crowned Henry II employed Iorwerth as an advisor on Welsh affairs; he was certainly used by Henry as an interpreter.

Madog soon came to realise that to rule Powys effectively he had to steer a middle course between the aggressive power of Gwynedd in the north and the threatening power of the Anglo-Norman Marcher lords in the east. Thus, while Madog threatened Shropshire, he negotiated an alliance with the ruler of the neighbouring county of Chester, Earl Ranulf. Ranulf's motive for securing an alliance with the ruler of Powys was two-fold: to avoid the fate of his neighbours in Shropshire, and to counter the threat posed by the growing power of Gwynedd under Owain Gwynedd. However, such was the threat posed by Gwynedd that Madog, no doubt following his brother Iorwerth's example, prepared to join the king of England, Henry II, in a military expedition against the men of Gwynedd. In 1157 Madog, together with his client Hywel ab Ieuaf of Arwystli, joined in Henry II's successful campaign against Owain Gwynedd. Madog's reward was both political and financial, for in supporting the king he acquired a guarantor of his kingdom's security along with substantial payments from the English exchequer.

Thereafter, from 1157 until his death in 1160, Madog ruled Powys unmolested. He was buried at a church, Meifod, that lay at the heart of his kingdom and which, according to the court poet Cynddelw, was well known as 'the burial-place of kings'. To the court poets Gwalchmai and Cynddelw, Madog was as brave and as generous as any of his princely contemporaries but it was his appreciation of fine poetry that most impressed them. Madog was a cultured man and although his prowess in battle was rightly lauded, his patronage of the arts and of the native church (there is no evidence that he patronised any of the continental monastic orders such as the Cistercians) was equally deserving of praise.

Politically as well as biologically (he is reported to have fathered as many as nine sons and four daughters) Madog's achievements were immense. He overcame familial strife, political difficulties and –

43

stuck between Gwynedd and England – geographical weakness to forge a secure and highly successful power base in Powys. He was a skilled political and diplomatic operator who formed alliances with Marcher lord, English king and Welsh prince with relative ease. In an effort to forge diplomatic and familial links with Deheubarth and Gwynedd he secured advantageous marriages for his daughters Gwenllian (who married the Lord Rhys of Deheubarth) and Marared (who became the wife of Iorwerth Drwyndwn ab Owain Gwynedd and thus the mother of Llywelyn ap Iorwerth).

Unfortunately, Madog's success in making Powys a strong, stable kingdom and a major player on the Welsh political scene did not long survive his death. Shortly afterwards his son and heir, Llywelyn, was killed. Described by the Welsh chroniclers as the one 'in whom lay the hope of all Powys', Llywelyn ap Madog's death marked the end of unitary rule in Powys. The kingdom was divided between Madog's three remaining sons Elise, Gruffudd Maelor (d. 1191), and Owain Fychan (d. 1187), his brother Iorwerth Goch, and his nephew Owain Cyfeiliog (d. 1197). Within a generation of his Madog's death Powys would be permanently divided into two competing kingdoms: Powys Wenwynwyn and Powys Fadog. From the latter kingdom would descend Owain ap Gruffudd Fychan, better known to history as Owain Glyndŵr.

Owain Gwynedd

Owain ap Gruffudd (d. 1170) – known to history as Owain
Gwynedd – prince of Gwynedd, was the second son of Gruffudd ap
Cynan and his wife, Angharad.

Owain first enters the historical record in 1124 when he and his
elder brother, Cadwallon, led a military expedition against
Meirionydd in 1124. Cadwallon's death in battle in 1132 left Owain
as his father's eldest surviving son and heir. Owain proved himself to
be a capable warrior and tactical commander and in 1136 he
ventured south to Ceredigion where he, and his younger brother
Cadwaladr, led two campaigns against the Anglo-Norman settlers in
Ceredigion.

On the death of his father, Gruffudd ap Cynan, in 1137 Owain
succeeded to the kingdom of Gwynedd, which he ruled until his own
death in 1170. In 1138 he returned to complete the conquest of
Ceredigion, which was divided between his eldest son, Hywel ab
Owain, and Cadwaladr. In this division of the spoils Owain was early
demonstrating his ruthless empire building, as he sought to exclude
the dynasty of Deheubarth from a share of Ceredigion – a territory
that, before its conquest by the Anglo-Normans, had long been part
of their patrimony.

On the other hand, Owain may have been pursuing a longer-term
goal of establishing his primacy over the other Welsh princes, for in
arranging the betrothal of his daughter to Anarawd, the son and heir
of the ruler of Deheubarth, Gruffudd ap Rhys, he was perhaps
intending to offer them a place in the new territorial arrangements
under his overlordship.

Unfortunately for Owain Gwynedd, his unpredictable brother
Cadwaladr had Anarawd murdered in 1143. A furious Owain
dispossessed his brother of his lands but the damage had been done.
The dynasts of Deheubarth no longer trusted those of Gwynedd and
any hope of a relationship between them was lost. In the meantime,
Owain found time to find a wife, and sometime in the early 1140s he
married Cristin, the daughter of Gronw ab Owain ab Edwin. Owain

and Cristin had three sons and a daughter, but it appears fidelity was not one of Owain's strengths since it is suspected that he had numerous other children with possibly as many as eight other partners, one of whom was an Irish woman called Pyfog.

His infidelities aside, the most damaging issue was the fact that Owain and Cristin were closely related, certainly within the prohibited degrees of marriage as defined by the Church. He was criticised for this by Giraldus Cambrensis, and though he was ordered to end his marriage by no less a person than Thomas Becket, Archbishop of Canterbury, Owain refused. For this, and for other examples of defiance, Owain was excommunicated. In an interesting postscript to this tale, eighteen years after Owain's death Gerald reported that while visiting Bangor, as part of his tour preaching the crusade, Baldwin, Archbishop of Canterbury, ordered the prince's body to be exhumed and buried in unconsecrated ground: needless to say his instruction was ignored.

Owain and Cadwaladr were reconciled in 1144 and together they embarked on an expansion programme which netted Gwynedd additional territories, most notably the lordships of Iâl and Tegeingl, and the building of castles such as at Tomen y Rhodwydd. These territories were won by bitter fighting that resulted in the defeat of the ruler of Powys, Madog ap Maredudd, and a temporary alliance with Ranulf, earl of Chester.

Having defeated his enemies and secured his political and territorial dominance in Gwynedd, Owain turned to dealing with his rivals within the kingdom. In 1152 he ran his brother Cadwaladr out of the kingdom and, in an act of ruthless barbarity, Owain had his nephew, Cunedda, the son of his deceased eldest brother Cadwallon, blinded and castrated. If the Welsh chroniclers are to be believed Owain, in stark contrast to his cruel treatment of his nephew, had a softer side to his character, for it is reported that on hearing of the untimely death of his young son Rhun in 1146, the prince broke down in tears and was for some time inconsolable.

Owain had become so powerful in Wales that he attracted the attention of the English king, Henry II. Only the king had the power and the resources to check Owain's territorial and political expansion. In 1157 the two clashed when Henry II led a military campaign to Wales to force Owain to submit to his authority. However, far from humbling the Welsh prince Henry's failed campaign added to Owain's growing reputation. The king's army failed to defeat Owain's troops, and a seaborne attack on Anglesey, an attempt to cut the Welsh off from their food supplies, ended miserably.

Ever the pragmatist, Owain realised that Henry II's superior resources and potential military strength would tell if a longer second campaign were planned and executed. Consequently, Owain was minded to submit and give homage to the king, but the price of peace was high: he had to surrender his conquests in Tegeingl, restore Cadwaladr to his lands, and refrain from any military activity that might upset the equilibrium in the March. This explains why Owain, if he could, turned to blinding and castrating his rivals so as to prevent them being used as pawns of an English king to curtail his authority.

In 1157 Henry received Cadwgan and Cynwrig, two of Owain's sons, as well as Maredudd, the son of the Lord Rhys, as hostages to the peace. In 1165, when Henry suffered losses at the hands of the Welsh on the Berwyn mountains, he removed the eyes of the young princes, split their noses, and filled their ears with wax. To complete the picture, two of Owain's sons were mutilated when held as hostages by the King of England (and Lord Rhys' nephew was killed).

Taking advantage of the constraints laid upon him by the king, Madog ap Maredudd's brother, Iorwerth Goch, attacked and destroyed the castle at Tomen y Rhodwydd and took back the lordship of Iâl. Revenge for Owain came three years later when, in 1160, he attacked Powys after hearing of the death of its ruler Madog ap Maredudd. The lordships of Edeirnion and Cyfeiliog were annexed, and in 1162 he led a punitive raid against Hywel ab Ieuaf, the ruler of Arwystli. To avoid retribution from Henry II in July 1163 Owain travelled to meet with the English king at Woodstock, where he again submitted and publicly acknowledged the overlordship of the Crown.

This renewed vow of submission lasted less than two years when Owain determined once and for all to throw off the English yoke. By threat and persuasion Owain managed to create an alliance of Welsh princes with him as its head. The rulers of Powys and Deheubarth joined Owain near the Berwyn Mountains in north Wales to await the invading English army. Henry II's campaign proved to be a disaster, coming to grief in the rain and mud of an unseasonally wet Welsh summer! Tired and disillusioned Henry II retired to the continent where he sought to re-shape his Welsh policy that only came to fruition after the death of Owain Gwynedd in 1170. With Owain's successor as premier Welsh prince, The Lord Rhys, Henry attempted to negotiate a settlement rather than militarily humble his opponent: it worked.

However, this was for the future and, in the meantime, Owain revelled in his position as the undisputed leader of native Wales, a supremacy he expressed by adopting a new title, namely, prince of the Welsh. So confident was he of his position in Wales that he became the first known Welsh ruler to seek and cement an alliance with the ruler of a continental power, namely, Louis VII, king of France. Louis was more than interested in cementing an alliance with a ruler who had defied his long-time enemy, the king of England, Henry II.

Although Owain failed to persuade Louis to make war on Henry II, he was not deterred from continuing the military campaign in Wales. In 1166–67 Owain re-took Tegeingl and captured the castles built by Henry II at Basingwerk, Rhuddlan and Prestatyn. Torn between keeping an eye on the French king Louis VII and the Welsh princes, Henry contented himself with a policy of containment. So long as Owain did not threaten the English border counties he was left to annex territories within Wales, this included the lands of other Welsh princes as well as Anglo-Norman Marcher lords. The latter were suitably unimpressed by their king's apparent indifference to their plight. The result was a series of marriage alliances between

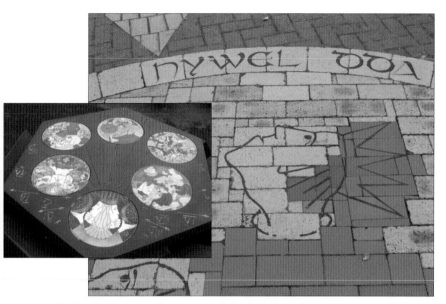

The Hywel Dda Memorial Gardens at Whitland, which mark the meeting convened by King Hywel in the mid tenth century to draw up The Law of Hywel (Cyfraith Hywel).

Rhuddlan castle was built in the thirteenth century by Edward I on the site of Gruffudd ap Llywelyn's timber and palisade court.

Carreg Cennen castle, built by Edward I on the site of the original Welsh fortress, probably built by one of the sons of the Lord Rhys.

The castle of Dinefwr, first mentioned in 1163 and located on an ancient site connected with the kingdom and princes of Deheubarth. The original may have been built by the Lord Rhys.

The castle at Cydweli was originally built by the Normans. It stands near the spot where Gwenllian, wife of Gruffudd ap Rhys and mother of the Lord Rhys, died in battle.

The first Welsh stone castle was said to have been built by the Lord Rhys at Cardigan (Aberteifi), on a bluff overlooking the river Teifi. It became his chief court, and here he held the first recorded Eisteddfod. His tomb is in St David's cathedral.

Dinas Brân castle was built by the Welsh princes of Powys Fadog sometime in the second half of the thirteenth century to dominate and control the Dee valley. It was built on the site of an old hillfort.

The princes of Gwynedd built Deganwy castle to defend the river crossing on the Conwy. It was built on an ancient site traditionally associated with Maelgwn Gwynedd.

Gruffudd ap Cynan was imprisoned in Chester for twelve years and was brought out of his dungeon to face mocking crowds outside the cathedral on market days. He escaped and returned to rule Gwynedd, driving out the Normans from the north west of Wales.

Ffordd y Saeson: an ancient trackway that was very likely used by invading English armies in Owain Gwynedd's time.

Owain Gwynedd was laid to rest in Bangor cathedral in 1170. Although he died excommunicate the bishop agreed to his burial on consecrated ground.

Dolwyddelan castle. Llywelyn Fawr is thought to have been born in the original castle in 1173.

Cricieth castle was built originally by Llywelyn Fawr, but after its capture by Edward I it was rebuilt and enlarged. Owain Glyndŵr's War of Independence saw the castle burned and the colonial town destroyed by Welsh forces.

A modern statue in the town square of Conwy depicting Llywelyn Fawr, who was buried in a monastery that occupied the site before the building of the modern town.

The tomb of Joan (or Siwan), daughter of the English King John and wife of Llywelyn Fawr, was originally in Llanfaes priory, but was moved to Beaumaris church.

During the Reformation, when Henry VIII closed the monasteries, the tomb of Llywelyn Fawr was plundered. The base of the tomb, minus the body and the coffin lid, was moved to the safety of Llanrwst church.

Offa's Dyke/Clawdd Offa (near Presteigne); built in the eighth century by King Offa of Mercia, and designed to define and defend the frontier between his kingdom and those of the Welsh.

The Offa's Dyke Path was established as a tourist attraction with a heritage centre at Knighton.

The ruins of the Cistercian monastery, Abbey Cwm Hir, lie in a remote valley near Builth Wells/Llanfair ym Muallt. It is said that on hearing of the death of Llywelyn apGruffudd in battle near Cilmeri the monks recovered the prince's body and, with the permission of Edward I, buried it within the abbey's precincts. A modern sculpted tomb marks the site

A memorial stone at Cilmeri, marking the site of the death of Llywelyn ap Gruffudd.

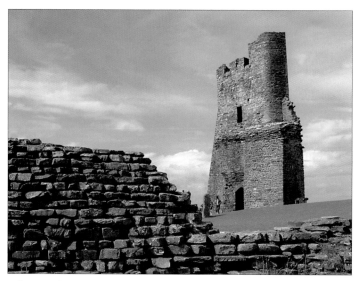

Aberystwyth castle was built by Edward I in the thirteenth century. It was captured by Owain Glyndŵr in 1404 and became an important centre of his power until its fall in 1408.

Built by Edward I in the thirteenth century, Harlech castle was captured in 1404 by Owain Glyndŵr and became the unofficial capital of his principality of Wales until it fell in 1409. Glyndŵr's flag flew proudly here, symbolising his power and authority: the four lions rampant of the Princes of Gwynedd.

The motte and bailey castle at Glyndyfrdwy was where the Glyndŵr rebellion began, when on 16 September 1400 Owain ap Gruffudd Fychan – Owain Glyndŵr – was declared Prince of Wales before his band of followers who went on to attack and burn the colonial town of Ruthin and ignite the War of Independence.

The Parliament House at Machynlleth. In 1404 Glyndŵr called his first parliament here, the first in Welsh history. Today it houses an Owain Glyndŵr exhibition, complete with a modern drawing of the prince fashioned from the wax seal image.

A modern bronze statue of Owain Glyndŵr erected in Corwen.

Above left: Owain Glyndŵr's flag, symbolising his power and authority: the four lions rampant of the Princes of Gwynedd. Above right: the wax seal of Owain Glyndŵr, an important tool of medieval government used to authenticate documents.

Pilleth/Pyllalai: the site of the battle of Bryn Glas, near the church just outside the village of Pilleth. Glyndŵr's men defeated an English army under Edmund Mortimer in June 1402.

The Pillar of Eliseg was set up near Llangollen by Cyngen, ruler of Powys, to honour and remember his great-grandfather.

Glyn y Groes (Valle Crucis) Abbey near Llangollen

The medieval monasteries of Strata Florida/Ystrad Fflur, Talyllychau and Valle Crucis/Glyn y Groes were either founded by or fully supported the native dynasties. Strata Florida became the dynastic mausoleum of the princes of Deheubarth, as did Valle Crucis for the princes of Powys Fadog.

Talyllychau

Stone memorial at Sempringham, Lincs, marking the life and death of Gwenllian, daughter of Llywelyn ap Gruffudd.

Llywelyn ap Gruffudd imprisoned Owain, his elder brother and rival, in Dolbadarn castle for twenty-two years.

Llywelyn's memorial at Caernarfon

Memorial statue to Llywelyn ap Gruffudd which stands in Llandovery/Llanymddyfri. He was executed for 'treason' in 1401. His sons were serving with Owain Glyndŵr.

Modern memorial erected in France to remember Owain ap Thomas ap Rhodri – Owain Lawgoch – a descendant of the last ruling dynasty of Wales. He was murdered by an English-paid assassin to prevent him from raising a rebellion in Wales.

Marcher and native princely families as the former sought their own means for survival.

Owain's confidence seemed to know no bounds for he was even prepared to defy a pope let alone an archbishop of Canterbury. When the latter demanded that bishops of Bangor swear allegiance to Canterbury and to the king of England, Owain protested and refused to allow the recently consecrated Meurig into Gwynedd to take up his office. In defiance of Owain's instruction to the contrary, Meurig had sworn allegiance both to the king and the archbishop, consequently he spent much of the remainder of his episcopate, from 1140 to 1161, in exile in England.

With Meurig's death Owain nominated Arthur of Bardsey to be the new bishop of Bangor an appointment Thomas Becket, the Archbishop of Canterbury, was happy to endorse so long as he, like his predecessor, accepted the authority of Canterbury and the Crown of England. Owain refused and is thought to have sent Arthur to Ireland to be consecrated bishop. Pope Alexander III weighed in on the side of Becket and ordered Owain, on pain of excommunication, to accept the archbishop's authority but he remained defiant. Attempts to resolve the dispute through the mediation of Louis VII came to nothing.

Owain died in November 1170. His achievements were considerable: he not only strengthened his kingdom but expanded it to embrace all of north Wales from the Dee to the Dyfi, thereby paving the way for the achievements of his grandson, Llywelyn ap Iorwerth. To his contemporaries he was, in the opinion of the Welsh chronicle *Brut y Tywysogyon* 'a man of great renown and of infinite prudence and nobility, the bulwark and strength of Wales'. Gerald of Wales praised him for his patronage of the Church, for his justice and wisdom, and in an echo of the flattering picture presented of him by the native annalists, he was described as a ruler who had died 'unconquered' by his enemies. To the poets like Gwalchmai ap Meilyr and Cynddelw Brydydd Mawr, Owain was 'the fairest of the kings of Britain', and in being among 'the most royal' he was eminently worthy to succeed great rulers such as Rhodri Mawr.

Unfortunately for Gwynedd Owain failed to ensure a smooth succession and shortly after his death his eldest son, Hywel ab Owain Gwynedd, who was most likely his chosen heir, was killed by his half-brothers Dafydd and Rhodri at the battle of Pentraeth in Anglesey. Consequently the kingdom was plunged into nearly three decades of conflict as the struggle for the control of Gwynedd among Owain's sons and grandsons intensified. It was only resolved with the ascendancy of Llywelyn ap Iorwerth in the early years of the thirteenth century.

Rhys ap Gruffudd

Rhys ap Gruffudd (c.1132–97), prince of Deheubarth, was also known as the Lord Rhys. He was the fourth of six sons born to Gruffudd ap Rhys (d. 1137) and Gwenllian (d. 1136), the daughter of Gruffudd ap Cynan, ruler of Gwynedd. He was the grandson of Rhys ap Tewdwr, the last king of Deheubarth before its destruction at the hands of Norman invaders. As the inheritor of his grandfather's greatness and his father's vision of a united kingdom free from foreign rule, much was expected of the young Rhys. The bards, those powerful propagators of populist propaganda, saw in him a man who, like Moses, would lead his people to the promised land of cherished independence from the yoke of Norman oppression.

Not that there was much hope of that ever happening when Rhys was born. Where once they had ruled a kingdom of forty commotes since the death of Rhys ap Tewdwr in 1093, the royal line of Deheubarth had been condemned to rule only the single commote of Caio. In a career spanning the best part of twenty-five years, Rhys's father and mother had fought and failed to restore the kingdom. Unlike most princesses of the time, his mother Gwenllian took up the cudgels of war and gave her life in battle, and in so doing sacrificed the lives of her two youngest children, one a babe-in-arms, to support her husband's desperate fight for freedom. On the death of Gruffudd ap Rhys in 1137 the mantle of leadership passed to his four remaining sons, Anarawd, Cadell, Maredudd and Rhys.

Anarawd was an early casualty of the struggle to restore Deheubarth when, in 1143, he was murdered not by his Norman enemies but by his father-in-law, and uncle, Cadwaladr ap Gruffudd of Gwynedd. Even in an age noted for its brutality Cadwaladr's treachery was reviled by contemporaries who condemned his attempt to wrest control of Ceredigion, one of the most prosperous parts of Deheubarth, from his hapless son-in-law.

In 1146, when he was fourteen years old, the chronicles first take note of Rhys who is described as scaling the walls of Llansteffan castle in support of his brothers. Thereafter, he is frequently recorded in their company on military expeditions mainly against the Normans in Dyfed (equating with modern Pembrokeshire) but also against his kinsman, Hywel ab Owain Gwynedd, in Ceredigion. Perceiving the slowly resurrecting Deheubarth to be ripe for plunder and dismember, some of the lesser princes of the dynasty of Gwynedd followed Cadwaladr's lead and fought for control of Ceredigion. Beset on all sides by enemies both Norman and Welsh, the sons of Gruffudd ap Rhys fought on regardless. However, in 1151 Cadell was seriously injured by a force of Normans operating out of Tenby who caught him hunting in the nearby forest of Coedrath (close to modern-day Saundersfoot). Left severely disabled by this encounter Cadell retired from the conflict and, sometime later, took up residence at Strata Florida abbey where he died in 1175. Maredudd followed him in 1155 when, at the age of twenty-five, he died of disease.

So from 1155, Rhys became the sole ruler of Deheubarth. The weight of expectation thrust on the shoulders of one so young might have daunted a man of lesser courage and spirit, but not Rhys. He had the good fortune to follow the example set by his parents and older brothers, who fell valiantly before him in the struggle to restore the ancient kingdom of Deheubarth to its former glory. Their sacrifice had not been in vain for Rhys inherited a kingdom comprising Ceredigion, Ystrad Tywi, and the greater part of Dyfed. The maintenance and consolidation of this restored kingdom was the principal objective of his reign.

During the first ten years of his rule, Rhys ap Gruffudd's fortunes were mixed. In 1156 he had to build a castle at Aberdyfi in order to defend the northern border of Ceredigion against his uncle, Owain Gwynedd. Rhys was also threatened by Henry II, recently established as king of England, who was determined to support the Anglo-Norman Marcher lords recover their lands in Wales. Between 1157 and 1162 Rhys was involved in almost continual warfare simply to survive, both personally and as ruler of Deheubarth. After the attack of 1162, two hostages were taken into the care of the Earl of

Gloucester – both were killed. In 1163 it seemed that luck had deserted him when he was captured and taken prisoner to England. At Woodstock in Oxfordshire, on 1 July 1163, Rhys was obliged to submit to Henry, accept his overlordship and his protection. His 'reward' was his release and the grant of Cantref Mawr with its castle of Dinefwr, the 'principal seat' of the kingdom of Deheubarth. The rest of his territory was parcelled out to the Anglo-Norman lords whom he and his brothers had dispossessed in the previous twenty years.

This setback proved only temporary, however, for in 1164 Rhys reconquered nearly all of Ceredigion. This was in revenge for the murder the previous year (probably during the prince's captivity in England) of his nephew, and chief of his 'teulu' or bodyguard, Einion ab Anarawd. Perpetrated by one of Einion's own men at the behest of Roger de Clare, the recently restored Anglo-Norman lord of Ceredigion, Rhys believed the crime had released him from his submission inasmuch as the king had failed to protect him and his family. Realising he needed allies if he was to challenge the king Rhys took advantage of his uncle Owain Gwynedd's quarrel with Henry II to form an alliance. Soon other princes joined the alliance, and at Corwen in 1165 they waited to resist Henry II's expected onslaught. Henry did not disappoint, and at the head of a formidable army he determined to crush the Welsh once and for all. Unfortunately for him the weather took an unexpected turn and drenched the heavily-laden invading army in a series of downpours which, allied to the difficult terrain and guerrilla tactics employed by the Welsh, forced him to retreat. Free from the threat of English interference (Henry II had problems elsewhere to deal with), Rhys completed his conquest of Ceredigion by capturing the castles of Cardigan and Cilgerran. The prince remained in possession of Ceredigion for the rest of his reign. Rhys's growing confidence in the security of his expanding kingdom enabled him to campaign further afield. In 1166–7 he joined Owain Gwynedd in military expeditions that led to the recovery of the lordship of Tegeingl for his uncle, and in the capture of the castle of Tafolwern and its lordship of Cyfeiliog for himself.

Up to 1171 Rhys's relations with Henry II were marked by defiance and hostility, punctuated by brief periods of reluctant compliance induced by the exercise or threat of English military force. From 1171 though, relations between the two rulers underwent a fundamental change. Aware that military solutions had failed to achieve stability in Wales, and fearful of the increase in Marcher power as a result of the conquests in Ireland, Henry II adopted a policy of *détente* with Rhys. In October 1171 Henry met Rhys at Pembroke, confirmed him in possession of the newly restored Deheubarth and released Rhys's son, Hywel Sais, whom he had held hostage since 1163. Evidently Hywel's eight-year detention had enabled him to learn the language of his captors – hence his nickname Sais (English-speaker). At Easter 1172 the king met Rhys again, at Laugharne, and, according to the Welsh chronicle the *Brut y Tywysogyon*, appointed him 'justice in all south Wales', thereby probably delegating authority to Rhys over the native rulers in Gwynllwg, Gwent, Glamorgan, Maelienydd, Gwrtheyrnion and Elfael.

1171–2 marked a turning point in Rhys ap Gruffudd's reign. It was the beginning of almost twenty years of largely uninterrupted peace with the English Crown and also the Marcher lords of south Wales. Rhys demonstrated his loyalty to Henry by sending his son, Hywel Sais, to assist the king in France during 1173–4, and Rhys himself led a force of his own on behalf of Henry at Tutbury in 1174. Between 1175 and 1185 Rhys met Henry II on no fewer than four occasions, during which relations between the two remained cordial in spite of tensions and threats to the peace caused mainly by disaffected Marcher and Welsh lords.

During this period of peace and increasing prosperity Rhys found time to indulge his passion for the opposite sex. He married Gwenllian, the daughter of Madog ap Maredudd, ruler of Powys, and also fathered some fifteen children, mostly illegitimate, and of whom the majority were boys a fact that would later come back to haunt him in his declining years. On a more morally dubious note Rhys is also said to have had a daughter by his own niece! Besides sex, castle-

building also preoccupied him during this time and there is evidence
to suggest that that he was responsible for erecting a number of stone
castles, the first of which was Cardigan in 1171.

The Church and religion too drew his attention as may be
witnessed in 1188 when he met the king's justiciar, Ranulf de
Glanville, together with Baldwin, Archbishop of Canterbury, at
Radnor at the start of the latter's journey round Wales to preach the
third crusade. Rhys later welcomed the Archbishop again at
Cardigan where he hosted him and his party within the walls of his
castle. Giraldus Cambrensis, who accompanied the Archbishop,
praised Rhys for his generosity, energy and wit, and suggests that the
prince would himself have taken the cross in 1188 had he not been
dissuaded by his wife. Whether Rhys was persuaded by the quality
and power of the preaching, or by religious zeal to risk his life
travelling to the Middle East and fighting the heathen Saracens to
free the Holy Land, is not known. In the event only a fraction of
those who took the cross and pledged to fight on behalf of the
Christian Church actually went to the Holy Land. Baldwin himself
travelled east only to die of disease.

Henry II's death in July 1189 marked the end of the largely
peaceful coexistence inaugurated in 1171–2. The last years of Rhys's
reign were dominated by renewed attacks on Marcher and royal
lands and castles in south Wales, due, largely, to his distrust of the
new king, Richard I, but also, in part, to satisfy the aggressive
ambitions of his sons. Rhys evidently considered his agreement with
Henry II to have been personal and no longer felt obliged to adhere
to its terms upon the king's decease.

By September 1189 his attacks on Crown and Marcher
strongholds provoked a royal expedition against him, the first for
over twenty years, under Richard I's brother, John, who concluded a
peace with Rhys and escorted him to the king at Oxford. However,
since Richard refused to see him, he was preoccupied with settling
his affairs in England so he too could join the third crusade, the
prince returned to Wales to continue his military campaign. Rhys
had troubles of his own and the ever-increasing rivalry between his

sons broke out into open conflict and by the end of 1189 the elderly prince had no choice but to imprison his eldest but illegitimate son, Malegwn, whom he later had transferred to the custody of his son-in-law, William de Braose. This left the way open for Rhys's legitimate son, Gruffudd, to succeed him.

In 1194, two years after his escape from prison, Maelgwn took his revenge on his father, whom he imprisoned in Nevern castle. Released by his other son Hywel Sais, Rhys determined to control his unruly sons, which he managed to do with difficulty by focusing on attacking their common enemy, the Anglo-Norman Marcher lords. In 1196 the old prince – then 64 – led his last major campaign, in which he burnt Carmarthen, defeated in battle one of the most powerful Marcher lords in mid-Wales, Roger Mortimer, and captured Painscastle, a fortress in the possession of his son-in-law, de Braose.

Rhys died, aged sixty-five, on 28 April 1197, and was buried in St. David's Cathedral. The tomb and effigy that shelters his body was added sometime in the fourteenth century.

Much of Rhys's fame and reputation rests upon his skill and success in warfare, which enabled him to restore and defend the kingdom of Deheubarth, over which he was the last native prince to exercise unitary rule. To the native poets and chroniclers Rhys was a 'second Alexander', an 'excellent protector', who 'defended the greatness of Deheubarth'. He was likewise described as the 'glory of Wales', and as 'the unconquered head of Wales'. However, he was more than simply a warrior dedicated to the art of war, for he was also a generous patron of the Church and native culture. Rhys patronized a wide variety of religious houses in Deheubarth but his especial treatment of the Cistercians played a crucial role in encouraging the spread of the order in native Welsh society. Rhys was also generous to poets, and the *Brut y Tywysogyon* describes a festival of music and poetry, often regarded as the first recorded eisteddfod, held by the prince in 1176 at his stone-built castle at Cardigan.

The fact of Rhys ap Gruffudd's willingness to live in peace

alongside the alien incomers, and his readiness to imitate Anglo-Norman fashions in castle-building and religious patronage, suggests he was a man at ease with the increasingly multi-cultural world in which he found himself. As such he stands as a model of successful integration for us today.

Owain Cyfeiliog

Owain ap Gruffudd ap Maredudd (d. 1197) was the son of Gruffudd
the brother of Madog ap Maredudd, prince of Powys. The identity
of Owain's mother is not certainly known, but is thought to have
been Gwerful the daughter of Gwrgenau from the region known as
Rhwng Gwy a Hafren. Known as Owain Cyfeiliog on account of his
having received this lordship from his uncle Madog ap Maredudd in
1149, it proved useful to distinguish him from his more famous
contemporary namesake, Owain ap Gruffudd or Owain Gwynedd.

Little is known of his early life or upbringing but whereas his
father and uncles had to fight to establish a landholding within the
kingdom of Powys Owain seems to have attracted the patronage of
his eldest uncle, Madog ap Maredudd, the ruling prince. It is possible
that Madog may have been impressed by his nephew's growing
reputation as a fierce warrior since Cyfeiliog lay at a critical strategic
junction between the lands of Gwynedd, Deheubarth and Arwystli.
As such it was prey to raids from its neighbours and whosoever
agreed to take power there would be expected to fight to retain
control. Thus as early as 1153 Owain Cyfeiliog was attacked by the
Lord Rhys of Deheubarth, who lay waste to the lordship before
withdrawing. Having recovered from this onslaught Owain was
confronted by Owain Gwynedd who not only attacked the lordship,
he ousted its lord, and took control there.

How and when Owain recovered the lordship is unknown but
there is evidence to suggest that he and his namesake, Owain
Gwynedd, effected a reconciliation through marriage. Owain's
marriage to Gwenllian, daughter of Owain Gwynedd, enabled him to
concentrate on fighting his Anglo-Norman neighbours to the east. In
1156 Owain led an assault on the earl of Chester's castle at Wrexham
in a successful attempt to rescue his brother Meurig from captivity.
The details of this expedition and the identities of those who took
part were famously captured in the epic poem *Hirlas Owain*.
According to Gruffydd Aled Williams, 'The 'Hirlas' is an unusual
poem, which, in dramatic style, depicts a feast in Owain's court' to

celebrate the success of the raid, during which 'Owain praises his brave warriors, calling upon his cup-bearer to bring the long blue ('hirlas') drinking-horn filled with mead to each hero in turn'.

Although Owain Cyfeiliog has long been acknowledged as the author of the poem, recent research has suggested that Madog ap Maredudd's court poet, Cynddelw Brydydd Mawr, may have been responsible for its composition. Whether he was the author or not, there is every reason to believe that Owain may have had a hand in composing songs and poems. It is generally agreed that Owain was a sensitive patron of the arts and literature, hence the reason why he occupies an honoured place in Welsh literary history. Cynddelw Brydydd Mawr was fulsome in his praise of Owain's largesse, in whose court 'there was drinking without want, without refusal'. Indeed, Giraldus Cambrensis praised the prince for his wit and 'the readiness of his tongue', but also for his 'justice, prudence, and moderation' as a ruler.

That he was a ruler of talent, whom the king of England took seriously enough to court as an ally, became apparent soon after the death of Madog ap Maredudd in 1160. Having become the dominant figure in a bitterly divided Powys, Owain set about the task of re-creating his uncle's authority by, firstly, claiming the princeship of the kingdom, and secondly, by crushing and expelling those who refused to accept his overlordship. The principal casualties of his ruthless rise to power were his uncle Iorwerth Goch, whom he ejected from the lordship of Mochnant, and his cousin Owain Fychan, whom he caused to be murdered (how is not known).

Within a few short years Owain successfully established himself as the undisputed ruler of the southern part of the kingdom (which became known as Powys Wenwynwyn after his son and heir) with his chief court at Welshpool. Aware of the strategic weakness of his kingdom Owain used diplomacy as effectively as war as a weapon to defend his patrimony. For example, when it suited his purpose in 1165 he joined his former adversaries, The Lord Rhys and Owain Gwynedd, in their war against the king of England, Henry II. However, once the threat of an English invasion had receded the

Welsh princes turned on each other, and, in 1167, both Owain Gwynedd and the Lord Rhys attacked Owain Cyfeiliog and took from him the lordship of Caereinion and the castle of Tafolwern. This explains why Owain sought to forge an alliance with his former enemy Henry II, to whose court he fled for protection.

Ever willing to stir the political and military pot in Wales, King Henry was more than happy to support the princely fugitive. With royal approval and Marcher support, Owain returned to Wales at the head of an Anglo-Norman and Welsh army. He won back the lands he had lost and destroyed the new castle his enemies had built at Caereinion. The conflict continued until at least 1171 when, after a second invasion of Powys by the Lord Rhys, Owain was forced to conclude a peace at the cost of surrendering seven hostages as a pledge of his good behaviour.

Thereafter, Owain enjoyed a period of peace and stability during which he cultivated a diplomatic, and personal, friendship with Henry II. Following a successful meeting with the king at Shrewsbury, Owain was later, in 1177, invited to attend the great council at Oxford, at which Henry II made his son, John, lord of Ireland. Together with other Welsh princes, including the Lord Rhys, he took an oath of fealty to Henry as his overlord. During this period of peace and prosperity Owain found time to found the Cistercian monastery of Strata Marcella near Welshpool.

Owain's generous endowment of the church, though, did not extend to his meeting Archbishop Baldwin of Canterbury during his crusading tour of Wales in 1188, accompanied by Giraldus Cambrensis. Baldwin's aim was to recruit troops for the forthcoming crusade to Palestine to eject the heathen arab, led by the formidable leader Saladin, from the Holy Land. However, Owain Cyfeiliog was the only Welsh prince who made no effort to meet the archbishop, let alone encourage his people to hear him preach, for which he was excommunicated.

As Owain grew older his sons, Gwenwynwyn and Cadwallon, assumed a greater share of their father's military and leadership role. In 1197, old and sick, Owain assumed the monastic habit of the

Cistercians and retired to die at the monastery of Strata Marcella; he was buried near the high altar. Owain was an independently-minded ruler who was lauded by the Welsh as a brave warrior and talented leader. To his Anglo-Norman neighbours he was remembered, in the thirteenth-century Anglo-French romance *Fouke le Fitz Waryn*, as 'a bold and fierce knight'.

Ifor (Bach) ap Meurig

Ifor ap Meurig (*fl.* 1150–74) (popularly known as Ifor Bach – Ifor the little) was a nobleman of obscure origins. Little is known of Ifor's dynasty but it seems that Ifor and his father, Meurig, emerged into notice out of the lesser nobility of Glamorgan during the reign of King Henry I. Glamorgan (or Morgannwg) was, along with Gwent, among the first of the Welsh kingdoms to be conquered and settled by the invading Normans late in the eleventh and early in the twelfth century. The killing and displacement of the members of the royal dynasty enabled noblemen like Ifor's father Meurig to establish themselves in smaller power blocks centred on lands located in the generally inaccessible upland regions of Glamorgan. Ifor was certainly an important lord of upland Glamorgan in the reign of Stephen (1135–54). He based his power in the lordship of Senghennydd, between the sons of Iestyn ap Gwrgant, the last independent ruler of Morgannwg, to the west, and that of Morgan ab Owain ap Caradog of Caerleon to the east. Unfortunately for Ifor Bach his neighbours, though Welsh, were as hostile to him as his natural enemy to the south, the Anglo-Norman lords of Cardiff. In his struggle for survival Ifor was forced to take some extraordinary risks, the story of which has made him something of a celebrity among the native rulers of medieval Wales.

In the opinion of the eminent historian, Sir John Edward Lloyd, 'a dramatic incident of the year 1158 deserves to be recorded, not only for its own sake, but also as an illustration of the irrepressible spirit of independence which still lived in districts supposed to be completely subjugated' to Anglo-Norman baronial power. Lloyd is referring to the daring night raid by Ifor Bach on Cardiff castle, where William, earl of Gloucester, his wife Hawise and their young son Robert were in residence. Protected by a strong garrison of mercenary troops, Ifor and his men scaled the walls and abducted William and his family, holding them hostage in the hills until his terms for a settlement were reached. Ifor demanded that the earl's attack on Senghennydd be abandoned, that the lands filched from him by the Anglo-Normans be restored to him and that additional territories be bestowed upon him by way of compensation. As far as is known the terms were met and the earl and his family were released.

Ignored by the native chroniclers but recorded by Giraldus Cambrensis, Ifor Bach's exploits were the stuff of legend. Gerald was clearly impressed by Ifor's daring adventure but the native chroniclers were only interested in recording the fact that in the same year Morgan ab Owain of Caerleon was 'slain through treachery by the men of Ifor ap Meurig, who was also credited with the killing of 'the best poet that was: Gwrgant ap Rhys'. It is perhaps a measure of Ifor's political and military success that he was courted by the Lord Rhys of Deheubarth, and had a marriage arranged between him and Rhys's sister, Nest.

Ifor's son and heir, Gruffudd ab Ifor (d. 1210), had succeeded his father by 1175, when, as Gruffudd ab Ifor ap Meurig of Senghennydd, he accompanied his uncle, the Lord Rhys, to Henry II's court at Gloucester. Thereafter the dynasty of Ifor Bach slipped slowly and quietly into obscurity.

Rhys Gryg

Rhys Gryg (d. 1233), a younger son of Rhys ap Gruffudd, was a prince who might have played a greater role in Welsh affairs had he succeeded as sole heir to his late father's kingdom. Unfortunately for him, when the Lord Rhys died so did the integrity of Deheubarth, which was partitioned between the old prince's various and quarrelsome sons.

The Lord Rhys's designated heir, Gruffudd ap Rhys, died within four years of his father, to be succeeded by his rival half-brother Maelgwn. The struggle to succeed to the headship of Deheubarth was long and bitter, but remained unresolved until the rising power of Gwynedd under Llywelyn ap Iorwerth took charge of the destiny of Deheubarth. Of all the sons of the Lord Rhys, Rhys Gryg alone maintained his grip on the ancestral heart and capital of the kingdom of Deheubarth, Ystrad Tywi and Dinefwr.

In the opinion of historian R. T. Jenkins, Rhys Gryg 'was an unreliable man, who rebelled against his father, played off one of his brothers against another, and played off King John against Llywelyn ap Iorwerth'. If he was guilty of being a 'self-seeker' then he was just one in an age of self-seekers, but Rhys was rather better at it than most of his contemporaries. His limited inheritance constrained his ambition and informed his actions. He was in a difficult position beset on all sides by enemies both real and imagined.

The most dangerous and aggressive of those enemies were members of his own close and extended family. His long-term ambition may have been to re-assemble the kingdom of his father with him as its prince, but reality ensured that his overriding aim was simply to survive and hang on to what he had. He was a brave and capable soldier and his military campaigns were generally successful but he lacked the authority and wider success necessary to establish his authority over Deheubarth.

With the benefit of the support of Llywelyn ap Iorwerth, prince of Gwynedd, Rhys vigorously contested possession of Ystrad Tywi and the key castles of Dinefwr and Llandovery. However, when

Llywelyn found himself under attack from King John in 1211 Rhys changed sides and supported the crown. His reward proved rather less than he had hoped when it became clear that the lands of his nephews was to be taken by the king instead of being given to him. Rhys promptly changed sides again and re-joined Llywelyn, during which campaign he captured and burnt the castle at Abersytwyth.

It was only in 1215 that the rivals for the supremacy in Deheubarth were reconciled when, for the first time, all the surviving descendants of Rhys ap Gruffudd were allied with Llywelyn against John. The crown's withdrawal from those parts of Wales claimed by Llywelyn added to the latter's power and prestige. Henceforth the likes of Rhys Gryg would have to seek their fortune in the courts of Gwynedd rather than at the palaces of the king of England.

At a gathering at Aberdyfi in 1216 Deheubarth was partitioned. Rhys Gryg won the main part of Ystrad Tywi, including the castle of Dinefwr, while his nephews, the sons of Gruffudd ap Rhys, secured the greater part of Ceredigion, and Maelgwn, Rhys's elder brother, received lands in Dyfed. The high point of Rhys Gryg's military career came in 1217 when, according to the *Brut* he

> overthrew Seinhenydd [Swansea] and all its castles to the ground. And he drove all the English away from that land [Gower] and took from them their chattels as much as he pleased; and he drove with them their wives and children without a hope of their ever returning. And he divided their lands for Welshmen to occupy.

Not that this episode of ethnic cleansing deterred Rhys from taking as his second wife the daughter of the Anglo-Norman earl of Clare!

For the rest of his life Rhys remained tolerably loyal to Llywelyn and but for an embarrassing episode in 1227 when he was imprisoned by his own son, he maintained his hold on Ystrad Tywi and Dinefwr. Rhys's death in 1233 at Llandeilo may have been caused by a wound sustained in the siege of Carmarthen castle which, if so, would have gladdened the heart of this old warrior. That he chose to be buried, as the *Brut* put it, 'near the grave of the Lord Rhys, his father', at St. David's cathedral says much about his pride, status and his unfulfilled life-time ambition.

Llywelyn ap Iorwerth

Llywelyn ap Iorwerth (c.1173–1240), prince of Gwynedd, also known as Llywelyn Fawr (or 'the Great') was the son of Iorwerth Drwyndwn (one of the sons of Owain Gwynedd), and his cousin Marared, the daughter of Madog ap Maredudd, prince of Powys. He was born in or about the year 1173. Tradition locates his birthplace at Dolwyddelan in Nant Conwy. Although his upbringing is shrouded in mystery, it is possible to speculate that after his father's early death he was taken by his mother to Powys where he was educated and trained.

According to the poet Prydydd y Moch, Llywelyn was no more than ten years old when he embarked on a military career, and Giraldus Cambrensis described Llywelyn as being around twelve years of age when he left Powys to involve himself in a bitter civil war for control of Gwynedd.

Between 1194 and 1195 he sided first with his uncle Rhodri, to defeat and expel his other uncle Dafydd from eastern Gwynedd (Rhodri and Dafydd were the sons of Owain Gwynedd). After this, he turned on his erstwhile ally, Rhodri, by siding with his cousins, the sons of Cynan ab Owain Gwynedd. In two hard-fought battles Rhodri was defeated by Llywelyn and ejected from his lands in western Gwynedd. Rhodri's death in 1195 was followed, in 1197, by Llywelyn's capture and imprisonment of Dafydd who later died in exile in England in 1203.

In 1198 Llywelyn turned to deal with his cousins, Gruffudd and Maredudd, sons of Cynan ab Owain Gwynedd. Gruffudd was defeated in battle early in 1199 while Maredudd was forced to submit and accept Llywelyn's authority. During this time Llywelyn may have married Tangwystl, daughter of Llywarch Goch, but if he did so their union was not recognised by the Church. At least two children, Gruffudd and Gwenllian, were born of this early relationship.

Llywelyn became sole ruler of Gwynedd in 1199. His ambition is made clear in two charters he issued to the Cistercian abbey at

Aberconwy in which he styled himself 'Prince of all north Wales'. He was determined that no-one should have the opportunity to do as he had done; those who dared challenge his authority were ruthlessly crushed. After accusing his cousin, Maredudd ap Cynan ab Owain Gwynedd, of treachery, Llywelyn removed him from Llŷn and Eifionydd. By 1201 Llywelyn had become undisputed prince of Gwynedd.

Having secured his position in north Wales, Llywelyn turned his attention towards the rest of Wales and beyond. His first act was to gain the friendship and support of King John of England, who recognised Llywelyn's position as ruler of Gwynedd and confirmed him in the possession of his lands. In 1201 Llywelyn and John entered into a more formal relationship by agreeing to a treaty, the first of its kind between a Welsh prince and an English king. According to the terms of the treaty Llywelyn, and the other princes of Wales, swore fealty to John and undertook to pay him homage on his return from France.

In the Spring of 1205, some six months after John's return from a disastrous continental campaign which witnessed the loss of much of his French lands, Llywelyn was offered the king's daughter, Joan, in marriage. Although Joan (known in Welsh as Siwan) was illegitimate, the fact remained that she was the king's daughter and Llywelyn knew that this union would elevate him and his dynasty to a higher status than that enjoyed by the other Welsh princely houses. As another sign of royal favour John presented his son-in-law with the valuable manor of Ellesmere in Shropshire.

Marriage was the norm in cementing political and military alliances at the time. The Welsh Princes regularly used this as a means to calm tension, create alliances, seal agreements and transfer land. It did not always guarantee peace or familial harmony, as Llywelyn was to find out later, but it did create a framework within which the warring parties could operate and keep in contact.

Llywelyn next turned his attention to mid and south Wales where he determined to extend his power and authority. In 1208 an opportunity presented itself when Gwenwynwyn of Powys, his princely neighbour and one-time enemy (they had clashed in 1202) fell foul of King John. Charged with an unprovoked attack on a Marcher lord, John confiscated Gwenwynwyn's lands. Llywelyn moved quickly to take control of Gwenwynwyn's principality of southern Powys and then he moved to seize those lands ruled by his enemy's princely allies – most notably, Maelgwn ap Rhys of Ceredigion.

Fortunately for Llywelyn John did nothing to stop his son-in-law's blatant empire-building – in fact, he seemed to approve, for in 1209 Llywelyn was invited to join his father-in-law's military campaign against William the Lion, king of Scotland.

This was the high-water mark of Llywelyn's cordial relations with King John. In 1210 relations soured when Llywelyn unwisely took advantage of John's absence in Ireland to support the fugitive Marcher lord, William de Braose, whom the king had earlier declared to be a traitor. Buoyed by his success in Ireland John determined to deal with his errant son-in-law and in 1211 two royal expeditions were launched against Llywelyn. In the face of such overwhelming power Llywelyn, with the aid of his wife, submitted to John. Acting as her husband's intermediary, Joan met her father and succeeded in persuading him to spare Llywelyn the humiliation of being removed as prince of Gwynedd. Nevertheless, Llywelyn was forced to surrender almost half his territory and also his son Gruffudd (son of Tangwystl), who became a hostage of the king.

However, Llywelyn's fortunes changed for the better in 1212 when John's pressure on the other Welsh princes drove them into the arms of the prince of Gwynedd, who led them in a successful campaign against the Crown. Distracted by his troubles in France John was hardly in a position to resist the Welsh, who were impressed by Llywelyn's statesman-like leadership. In 1212 Llywelyn became the first Welsh prince to conclude a treaty of alliance with a foreign power in the shape of the French king, Philip Augustus. The Pope, Innocent III, also offered his support to Llywelyn by absolving the Welsh prince from all his promises and oaths of fealty to John.

By 1215 Llywelyn's war against John had spilled over into England when the barons, too, turned on their king and forced him to sign Magna Carta. It is a measure of Llywelyn's success that in aligning himself with the rebel English barons the Welsh prince was able to win concessions that were recorded in the Great Charter. In 1216 Llywelyn exercised his power by summoning all the other princes of Wales to a meeting at Aberdyfi. Not only was this a clear demonstration of his superior status and authority but he may well have extracted oaths of homage and obedience from his fellow Welsh princes.

His redistribution of the lands of the former kingdom of Deheubarth confirmed his power over native south Wales, while his seizure of southern Powys on the defection of Gwenwynwyn to John secured control of native mid-Wales. He occasionally had to lead military expeditions to punish his vassals, principally the errant princelings of the former Deheubarth, but, henceforth, Llywelyn's position as the premier prince in Wales was never seriously threatened.

The death of John in 1216, and the signing of a peace treaty at Worcester with his successor Henry III in 1218, confirmed Llywelyn's ascendancy in Wales. For the remainder of his life Llywelyn pursued two key objectives: to secure the recognition of his position as prince of Wales in a formal treaty with the king of England, and the undisputed succession of his son Dafydd by his wife Joan.

Llywelyn used any and all means at his disposal to achieve his twin objectives. He used war and, alternatively, marriage to pacify and conciliate his Marcher neighbours. He took the castle and lordship of Builth from the Braose family and the castles of Neath and Cydweli were captured from Hubert de Burgh. On the other hand, Dafydd was married to Isabella de Braose; Gwaldus to Reginald de Braose and afterwards to Ralph Mortimer; Margaret was married to John de Braose and afterwards to Walter de Clifford; Gwenllian married William de Lacy and Helen married John the Scot, the son of Llywelyn's closest ally, Earl Ranulf of Chester.

Llywelyn used diplomacy and persuasion to bring the English Crown to the negotiating table. After three failed royal expeditions to Wales in 1223, 1228 and 1231, Llywelyn arranged peace accords with the English king such as that at Middle in 1234, which virtually established peace for the remainder of his reign. Llywelyn arranged assemblies of his vassals, the princelings of Wales, for example at the Cistercian abbey of Strata Florida in 1238, during which he sought to bind them into an agreement recognising his son Dafydd as his heir. It has been suggested that Llywelyn may have intended to use this occasion to retire after delivering his power into the hands of his son. His wife Joan, on whom he had depended, had died the previous year, and he had suffered a stroke before the end of 1237.

It is perhaps a measure of the love he bore Joan that on hearing of her affair with William de Braose, Llywelyn cast aside his political cares to exact the revenge of a husband wronged by publicly hanging the perpetrator. The place of execution may be that still remembered locally as Gwern y Grog or Hanging Marsh. The *Brut y Tywysogyon* relates the story thus 'that year William de Breos the Younger, lord of Brycheiniog, was hanged by the lord Llywelyn in Gwynedd, after he had been caught in Llywelyn's chamber with the king of England's daughter, Llywelyn's wife'. Given the nature of the sources available to us, written in bare factual detail by closeted monks, it is the closest we can get to some understanding of the emotional lives lived by the people at that time.

Llywelyn died in April 1240 and he was buried in the Cistercian abbey at Aberconwy. Within months of his death it became clear that Llywelyn had failed to achieve his aims: Dafydd's claim to the kingdom of Gwynedd was challenged by his elder half-brother Gruffudd and civil war seemed likely. The lesser princelings renounced their agreement to recognise Dafydd as Llywelyn's successor and, with the support of the English Crown, took every opportunity to break away from Gwynedd's control. Nor did the English king ever formally recognise Llywelyn's claim to be prince of Wales. Indeed, Henry III did everything in his power to reduce the status and power of his son Dafydd.

Despite these setbacks, there is no doubt that Llywelyn ap Iorwerth stands out as one of the greatest rulers of native Wales. Having begun with next to nothing, he ended his reign as Prince of Wales in all but name. His adoption of the title 'Prince of Aberffraw and Lord of Snowdon' after 1230 is indicative of his aim to claim the princeship of Wales, a feat achieved by his grandson Llywelyn ap Gruffudd in 1267. Llywelyn changed the laws of Gwynedd to strengthen his position, he built castles to defend his expanding kingdom and he raised and led armies capable of resisting both Marcher lords and English kings alike. He brought the whole of native Wales under his control and ensured that, henceforth, the Welsh princelings had either to accept his lordship or that of a foreign English king.

Llywelyn was also a generous patron of Welsh culture and the Church. The poets, chief among them Cynddelw Brydydd Mawr, Dafydd Benfras and Llywarch ap Llywelyn (better known under the nickname *Prydydd y Moch*) appreciated his patronage and they eulogized him. The Church remembered him, particularly the English monk Matthew Paris who seems to have been the first to describe his 'Greatness'. Llywelyn's patronage of the religious orders was evident in his generous grants of land to monasteries at Cymer, Penmon and Aberconwy.

As a mark of his esteem for the monastic life, Llywelyn chose to be buried in the monastery he most cherished, Aberconwy. Today, the site is occupied by Conwy castle, whose builder, Edward I, was responsible for removing the abbey some ten miles down stream to Maenan. Llywelyn was re-buried at the new site and there he remained until the dissolution of the monasteries in the 1530s when his coffin was unceremoniously thrown into the river. His corpse was lost but the stone sarcophagus that held it was recovered, and is on display in Llanrwst church.

Llywelyn's achievements far outweigh his failures and there is no doubt that he deserves to be remembered as Llywelyn Fawr (or Llywelyn the Great).

Siwan (Joan) daughter of King John and wife of Llywelyn ap Iorwerth

Joan (known in Welsh as Siwan) (d. 1237) was the illegitimate daughter of John, king of England, and an unknown mother. Joan was the daughter of one of the most powerful kings in western Europe. Her father had inherited England, the overlordship of Ireland and Wales and the extensive power of the Angevin Empire which covered the greater part of France. By the time of her marriage in 1205 her father had lost control of the Empire, ceding much of his authority to the French king, Philip Augustus. Joan appears to have spent her formative years in France before embarking for England in 1203 aboard a ship arranged to 'carry the king's daughter' from Normandy. Her life had been predetermined by her father, who was intent on using her as a diplomatic pawn in international politics. Within a year of arriving in England she was being prepared for marriage and in October 1204 Joan was betrothed to Llywelyn ap Iorwerth, prince of Gwynedd. The couple married in the spring of 1205 and as part of her dowry, the castle and manor of Ellesmere was granted to Llywelyn by King John in April 1205.

Joan frequently acted as an ambassadress and intermediary between her husband and her father, John, and brother, Henry III, in the period 1209–1232. Her role as a mediator was crucial in the crisis of 1211 when her husband and father fell out and went to war. After John had conducted a successful campaign in north Wales against him the Brut states that 'Llywelyn, being unable to suffer the king's rage, sent his wife, the king's daughter, to him, by the counsel of his leading men, to seek to make peace with the king on whatever terms he could'. Llywelyn was obliged to hand over hostages, pay a heavy tribute of cattle, and cede half his kingdom of Gwynedd to John. In September 1212, when John was preparing another attack on Wales, Joan sent him a warning of treason among his barons, which induced the king to disband his invading army. In 1214 she negotiated with her father for some Welsh hostages in England, whose release she obtained within eighteen months of her intervention.

Joan continued her work of mediation after the accession of Henry III; a letter is extant in which she pleads earnestly with him for a good understanding between him and Llywelyn. In September 1224 she met Henry in person at Worcester, and in 1225 he granted her the manor of Rothley in Leicestershire, to be followed the next year by that of Condover in Shropshire. These lucrative grants of land mark the high point of her influence in English politics and in reward of her efforts to maintain good relations between the Welsh and English her brother, Henry III, persuaded Pope Honorius III to declare her to be of legitimate birth in 1226.

However, such was the fragility and fickleness of diplomatic relations early in 1228 the king took back the two manors, probably as a result of rising tension between Llywelyn and the king's chief adviser Hubert de Burgh. Joan met Henry at Shrewsbury that summer and arranged a truce, and the manors were restored to her in November. Her son Dafydd did homage to the king as Llywelyn's heir at Michaelmas 1229.

In April and May 1230 Joan was caught up in an affair that threatened to ruin her reputation and destroy her achievements. According to the *Brut* the Anglo-Norman lord William de Braose was 'caught in Llywelyn's chamber with the king of England's daughter, Llywelyn's wife'. The affair may have begun two years earlier in 1228 when de Braose, wounded and captured in battle, was conveyed to Gwynedd as Llywelyn's prisoner. William de Braose may have been nursed back to health by Joan, which would partly explain the background to their affair. After his release William had returned to Llywelyn and Joan's home to arrange a marriage between his daughter Isabella and Joan's son Dafydd. On discovering William and Joan's affair, an enraged Llywelyn quickly tried and executed de Braose, who was hanged in public at Crogen near Bala, in May 1230.

The affair had the potential to wreck Joan's marriage to Llywelyn, a man for whom she appears to have felt a genuine love and affection. That these feelings were reciprocated is indicated by the fact that after a short imprisonment of some twelve months, Joan and Llywelyn were reconciled in 1231. Seven hundred years later, the event found a place in modern Welsh literature when it was immortalised in the play *Siwan* (1956) by Saunders Lewis.

In 1232 Joan was one of a delegation sent by Llywelyn to meet Henry III at Shrewsbury. This was to be her last diplomatic foray on behalf of her adopted people, the Welsh. Joan died in February 1237 at the royal palace of Aber near Bangor. At the place of her burial, the royal manor of Llanfaes in Anglesey, Llywelyn founded a Franciscan friary in her memory. Her stone coffin, removed at the dissolution of the friary in the 1530s, was rescued from use as a horse-trough early in the nineteenth century. It can now be seen in the porch of Beaumaris church complete with a sculpted effigy of the princess.

Rhys ap Maredudd

Rhys ap Maredudd (d. 1292) was the son of Maredudd ap Rhys Gryg lord of Dryslwyn in Carmarthenshire, and Isabel, daughter of William Marshal, earl of Pembroke. Rhys ruled a small part of what was once the mighty kingdom of Deheubarth. His share of the patrimony was confined to the Tywi valley and some of the upland territories of Carmarthenshire.

Rhys was not without talent and he was a courageous soldier, but his ambition far outran his resources to fulfil it. He followed his father in rejecting the overlordship of Gwynedd under prince Llywelyn ap Gruffudd in favour of royal control. Like his father and grandfather before him, Rhys was a maverick who was determined to go his own way, but in the increasingly tense atmosphere of the latter half of the thirteenth century, caused by the rising power of Gwynedd and the growing hostility of the Marcher lords, he found himself caught between the two. When Llywelyn ap Gruffudd succeeded in persuading King Henry III to recognise him as Prince of Wales in the Treaty of Montgomery of 1267, alone of the lesser native princes Rhys's father refused to offer his allegiance to the Welsh prince, preferring instead the authority of the English crown. Much to Maredudd's anger and annoyance the crown sold his clientship to Llywelyn in 1270. This episode seems to have convinced Maredudd that neither side could be trusted, an attitude that came to be shared by his son Rhys.

Rhys succeeded his father in 1271. In 1276 when the new king, Edward I, went to war with Llywelyn, known as the First War of Welsh Independence, Rhys remained loyal to the English. In return for his loyalty Rhys came to an agreement with Edward I in 1277, in which he was promised Dinefwr Castle and the lands of his kinsman, Rhys Wyndod, once they fell into the king's hands; Rhys also agreed to do homage and publicly accept the king as his overlord. However, Rhys Wyndod soon submitted to the king and, like Rhys, swore homage to Edward; some of his estates were confirmed to him but Dinefwr Castle was seized by the king's lieutenant, Payn de

Chaworth. Rhys ap Maredudd's ambition to control the Tywi valley was thus frustrated. To make matters worse he was brought under closer royal control when Chaworth asserted the king's right of entry to Dryslwyn Castle and royal justices subjected Rhys to the king's court in Carmarthen. Despite the king's broken promise and the aggressive nature of royal authority in his domain, Rhys ap Maredudd, unlike his kinsmen, remained loyal to the crown.

When Edward I and Prince Llywelyn went to war in March 1282, Rhys's loyalty to the crown was put to the test once more. He was promised rewards of land and the possibility of being bestowed Dinefwr castle if he supported the king in the war. With the defeat and death of Llywelyn in 1282 the war drew to a close, and Rhys was delighted to be granted land in Ceredigion in addition to Rhys Wyndod's forfeited estates. As a sign of his complete complicity in the crown's actions in south Wales he even acted as the king's agent in receiving Welshmen into Edward's peace. However, when Edward discovered that Rhys had already occupied the lands granted to him their seizure was ordered and Rhys was arrested. The lands were restored to him in October 1283, but only after he was forced to renounce all claims to Dinefwr Castle, the object of his ambition. Once again the heavy hand of royal authority descended on Rhys and his domain, but he was powerless to act, and he had no choice but to accept his subservient position.

Rhys suffered in relative silence for four years until 1287 when he rebelled. By September 1286 it became clear that Rhys's relations with Edward I had deteriorated. The principal reason for this was the unreasonable behaviour of the royal justiciar of west Wales, Robert Tiptoft. Tiptoft proved harsh and inflexible in his attitude towards Rhys, who responded by refusing to attend the king's court in Carmarthen. As lord of Emlyn, where his father had built a new castle, Rhys claimed that he was not subject to the king's justiciar at Carmarthen but rather to the Pembroke county court. The king was prepared to investigate the claims and accusations of Rhys and Tiptoft, but Rhys did not trust him. Rather than appear before the royal justices at Carmarthen he attacked and captured the castles of

Dinefwr, Carreg Cennen and Llandovery.

With the king away in France, his brother Edmund, earl of Cornwall, was ordered to put down the revolt and seize Rhys's possessions. By the first week in August 1287 a massive English army of over 25,000 men, divided into four units, converged on Carmarthen. Subduing the countryside as they marched, the army, under Earl Edmund, began its assault on Rhys's fortress of Dryslwyn, with siege equipment shipped from Bristol.

The siege lasted three weeks, during which mining beneath the castle chapel led to a roof collapse that killed some leading commanders. Rhys escaped, though most of his supporters surrendered. In September the stronghold of Newcastle Emlyn was also captured, but Rhys evaded capture.

In November 1287 Rhys suddenly attacked and captured Newcastle Emlyn, and Llandovery was sacked days later. In December steps were taken to recover Newcastle Emlyn, and the great siege-engine used at Dryslwyn was dragged to the castle. Within ten days the castle surrendered. Rhys again escaped, with a price on his head.

Eventually, on 2 April 1292, he was betrayed in the Tywi valley by some of his own men. Rhys ap Maredudd was sent in chains to Edward I at York, where he was convicted of murder, arson, theft, and the destruction of royal castles; he was hanged on 2 June. His son and heir Rhys was arrested and imprisoned in Norwich Castle where he remained until at least 1340. Rhys's rebellion led to the completion of the English conquest of south-west Wales and to the end of princely rule in Wales.

Gruffudd ap Gwenwynwyn

Gruffudd ap Gwenwynwyn (d. 1286), prince of Powys Wenwynwyn, was the son of Gwenwynwyn, the son of Owain Cyfeiliog and Margaret Corbet. Unfortunately for Gruffudd, his father, Gwenwynwyn, failed to maintain the family's hold on the Powys bequeathed by Owain Cyfeiliog. This led to Gruffudd being brought up in exile in England where he grew to manhood with a burning desire to recover the family's patrimony.

Gwenwynwyn's tenure as prince of Southern Powys began brightly enough: he succeeded his father, Owain Cyfeiliog, unchallenged, and was successful in stamping his authority throughout the region. His leadership qualities and skills as a warrior were praised by the poets, who claimed that he was the equal of his father. With much to live up to, Gwenwynwyn served notice that he was determined to carve out his own niche in Welsh political history. Taking advantage of the death of the Lord Rhys in 1197 and the subsequent disunity that tore the dynasty of Deheubarth apart, Gwenwynwyn set out to establish his leadership of the Welsh princes. He was helped in the fact that the dynasty of Gwynedd, too, was divided between the warring sons of the deceased Owain Gwynedd, namely, Rhodri and Dafydd.

However, the rise of the young Llywelyn ap Iorwerth in Gwynedd, and the unpredictable nature of King John's attitude to the Welsh princes in general, and Gwenwynwyn in particular, soon conspired to hinder Gwenwynwyn's progress to greatness. His ill-advised attacks on Marcher territories along the rivers Severn and Wye proved militarily disastrous. With his military reputation severely dented by these failures, his political instincts also deserted him when he failed to appreciate the king's determination to curtail his adventures in the March. In 1208 the king deprived him of his lands and he was reinstated only in 1210, when John required an ally against the rising power of Gwynedd in the shape of Llywelyn ap Iorwerth.

Gwenwynwyn found himself caught between John on the one

hand and Llywelyn on the other, but the proximity of the latter caused the prince of Powys to side with the prince of Gwynedd when war with the English seemed inevitable. However, Gwenwynwyn proved an unreliable ally, and when Llywelyn felt strong enough to conduct his campaigns without his aid Powys was invaded and its prince ejected. In the opinion of T. Jones Pierce, Gwenwynwyn's lasting legacy was to leave a 'permanent stamp of the nomenclature of central Wales' in the form of Powys Wenwynwyn.

After fleeing to England in 1216, Gwenwynwyn died later that same year to be succeeded by his son Gruffudd. Gruffudd survived on the income from his mother's English estates and on the charity of John's successor as king, Henry III. Llywelyn kept Powys Wenwynwyn in his hands until his death in 1240. When Llywelyn's heir, Dafydd, submitted to Henry III in 1241, the king took advantage of the Welsh prince's weakness to restore Gruffudd ap Gwenwynwyn to his father's patrimony. During this time, probably before 1242–3, Gruffudd married Hawise, the daughter of John Lestrange of Knockin. Hawise outlived her husband by over twenty years, dying in 1310 after having given birth to at least six children: five boys, and a girl, Margaret.

When war broke out between Dafydd and Henry III in 1244, Gruffudd ap Gwenwynwyn alone remained faithful to the king when the other princes sided with the prince of Gwynedd. He was besieged in his castle of Tafolwern but he survived to lead an army north to ravage Gwynedd after Dafydd's death in 1247. Between Dafydd's death in 1247 and the succession of his nephew Llywelyn ap Gruffudd in 1255, Gruffudd enjoyed a period of relative peace and stability. Indeed, his fidelity to the English king brought him more privileges and grants from the Crown.

However, with Llywelyn ap Gruffudd's rise to ever greater power and prominence in Wales Gruffudd soon found himself at odds with the new ruler of Gwynedd. Like his father and grandfather before him, Gruffudd had to walk a political and diplomatic tightrope between the rulers of Gwynedd and England. Unfortunately for him, Gruffudd soon found himself in conflict with a prince of Gwynedd who, like his grandfather before him, Llywelyn ap Iorwerth, had ambitions of becoming Prince of Wales. Gruffudd was unwilling to submit to Llywelyn ap Gruffudd's authority, and was attacked in 1257 – and again in 1258 when he was deprived of his patrimony.

Like his father, Gruffudd took refuge in England and in 1260 he agreed to serve in a military expedition against Llywelyn. Failing to achieve the success he expected, Gruffudd made his peace with Llywelyn in 1263 and, on bended knee, did homage to him as Prince of Wales, receiving in return some additional grants of territory. In 1267 Gruffudd, no doubt with much displeasure, had to witness the signing of the treaty of Montgomery in which the Crown formally recognised Llywelyn as Prince of Wales. Jealous and resentful Gruffudd plotted with Llywelyn's brother Dafydd to assassinate the prince: should they succeed, Dafydd would become prince and one of his daughters would marry Gruffudd's eldest son Owain, while Gruffudd himself would receive the territories of Ceri and Cedewain to add to his patrimony of Powys Wenwynwyn.

But the plot failed. In 1274 Gruffudd was forced to seek Llywelyn's pardon and hand over Owain as a hostage. Owain's confession as to the substantial part his father played in the plot caused Llywelyn to send a delegation to Gruffudd to answer further charges. Clearly worried by the implications of this turn of events, Gruffudd imprisoned Llywelyn's men and fled to join Dafydd in England. Llywelyn attacked and annexed Powys Wenwynwyn but his hold on Gruffudd's territory lasted only three short years.

The outbreak of war between King Edward I and Llywelyn in 1276 and the latter's defeat in 1277 enabled Gruffudd to reclaim his patrimony. Henceforth he remained faithful to King Edward, whom he supported when war with Llywelyn was renewed in 1282. The fall of Llywelyn in 1283 left him as undisputed master of Powys Wenwynwyn but, henceforth, he had to drop any pretension to being a Welsh prince and be content to play the part of an English baron. In 1283 he was summoned to the royal council which tried and sentenced to death his former ally, Dafydd, at Shrewsbury.

Gruffudd died in 1286 to be succeeded by his eldest son and heir

Owain. His heir, Owain de la Pole (after the castle of *Welsh*pool), as he came to be called, died in 1293, to be succeeded by his two-year-old son and heir, Gruffudd. On his death in 1309 Powys went to his sister, Hawise, who in the same year married John Charlton, who became the first Baron Charlton of Powys.

Llywelyn ap Gruffudd

Llywelyn ap Gruffudd (d. 1282), prince of Wales, was the second of four sons of Gruffudd ap Llywelyn (d. 1244) and his wife, Senana, and grandson of Llywelyn ap Iorwerth.

During the reign of his uncle Dafydd ap Llywelyn (1240–46), Llywelyn learnt first hand what it meant to be a ruler in Wales. With a ruthless disregard for familial loyalty the young Llywelyn did nothing to oppose his uncle's arrest and imprisonment of his father Gruffudd and elder brother Owain. Indeed, the fact that Llywelyn was allowed to remain free and was to be found in his childless uncle's company suggests that he was not only favoured but may even have been designated as heir.

When in 1244 war broke out between Dafydd ap Llywelyn and Henry III, Llywelyn repaid his uncle's treatment of him by supporting him in the conflict. When Dafydd died without an heir in 1246 Llywelyn assumed his place as ruler of Gwynedd. The return of his elder brother Owain from exile in England, to where he had been sent by Dafydd, may have hindered Llywelyn's quest for the undisputed leadership of Gwynedd but it did not stop it. Sponsored by King Henry III, who had a vested interest in keeping the Welsh princes weak, Llywelyn and Owain met at Woodstock in 1247 and agreed to divide Gwynedd between them.

The weakness of their uncle's position at his death was apparent for all to see when the king kept possession of half of Gwynedd (east of the Conwy known as the Perfeddwlad). The remainder, west of the Conwy (known as Gwynedd Uwch Conwy and centred on Snowdonia and Anglesey) was left to Dafydd's successors, Owain and Llywelyn. Within six years of the treaty of Woodstock their brother Dafydd ap Gruffudd was asserting his right to a share of the inheritance. Supported by Henry III Owain reluctantly agreed to a further division of the patrimony, but Llywelyn refused.

Civil war followed when in 1255 Owain and Dafydd were defeated by Llywelyn at the battle of Bryn Derwin. The defeated brothers were imprisoned, and Llywelyn took control of the whole of

Gwynedd Uwch Conwy. Keen to recover the rest of Gwynedd, in 1256 Llywelyn attacked the English garrisons in the Perfeddwlad and took it from the Crown. Only the castles of Diserth and Deganwy held out for the king, but their isolation was complete when they were besieged by the Welsh. By 1257 Llywelyn had succeeded in reassembling the patrimony of his grandfather Llywelyn the Great.

Unwilling to share his kingdom with his siblings Llywelyn kept Owain under lock and key but released Dafydd. In a clever piece of politicking Llywelyn invested Dafydd with a substantial landholding in the Perfeddwlad with the aim of detaching his brother from his alliance with Henry III. By giving him property once held by the king, Llywelyn calculated that his brother would now have to defend it from his erstwhile ally. Why he did not keep Dafydd incarcerated remains a mystery, but having no wife or children of his own perhaps Llywelyn intended that his younger brother should succeed him if he died.

In the following five years Llywelyn succeeded in establishing a broad supremacy over the lands of other Welsh rulers: in Deheubarth he won the support of Maredudd ab Owain and Maredudd ap Rhys Gryg, and in Northern Powys (or Powys Fadog) he was supported by Gruffudd ap Madog. So secure was he that in 1258 Llywelyn held an assembly of the lesser princes and most powerful magnates of Wales who swore oaths of allegiance to him. With their pledges of loyalty, and with the support of the bishops of Bangor and St Asaph, Llywelyn felt confident enough to formally and publicly style himself Prince of Wales, the first Welsh ruler to do so. Dafydd, and the ruler of Southern Powys, Gruffudd ap Gwenwynwyn, were unimpressed by Llywelyn's new-found authority, as was the English king, but with problems aplenty in England he could do nothing.

Llywelyn was not just a warrior: his martial prowess was beyond reproach, he was also a skilled and astute politician who was aware of how powerful a weapon diplomacy could be when used properly. Consequently, in a clear demonstration of his political vision

Llywelyn spent the next nine years (1258–67) in a quest for a peace treaty that would not only encourage the king to recognize his dominance in Wales but regulate his relationship with the Crown. Llywelyn wanted the king of England to recognise that Wales was a nation separate from England with its own laws and system of government. Henry III was naturally against any such recognition since it would threaten his dominance in Wales whilst encouraging the formation of a potentially hostile independent state on England's western border.

However, confronted by baronial opposition led by Simon de Montfort, Henry found himself in a difficult position. Those barons who supported him against de Montfort, were, for the most part, Marcher lords, several of whom had been victims of Welsh aggression, who would violently oppose any such parley or agreement with their greatest enemy Llywelyn. To encourage the king to decide in his favour and sign an agreement Llywelyn launched an attack upon the royal castle of Builth in 1260 to coincide with renewed diplomatic initiatives. Llywelyn's twin policy of diplomacy and military aggression failed to move the king but it did have the unintended effect of encouraging his brother Dafydd to defect to the Crown.

Sensing Llywelyn' failure to pin the king to an agreement Dafydd might have reasoned that his brother's power and influence would soon wane: he was wrong. Llywelyn changed direction and sided with the baronial opposition under de Montfort at which time he cemented his relationship by promising to take his ally's daughter, Eleanor, to be his wife. This was a clear demonstration to the king that Llywelyn was serious in his support of de Montfort and that any future agreement with the Crown of England regarding his position in Wales would include the baronial opposition. Unlike Dafydd Llywelyn's other opponent within Wales, Gruffudd ap Gwenwynwyn, was realistic enough to see that the Crown could do little to dislodge the Welsh prince and in 1263 he reluctantly agreed to submit himself to the self-styled 'Prince of Wales'.

When civil war broke out in England in 1264 Llywelyn sent

military aid to the baronial opposition under his future father-in-law, de Montfort. Together they attacked Radnor castle and marched on Montgomery and later Worcester. Success seemed at hand when de Montfort defeated and captured both Henry III and his son Prince Edward. However, Edward soon escaped and continued the war, freeing his father and defeating de Montfort's army, which included a sizeable Welsh contingent, at the battle of Evesham in 1265. With de Monfort's death the king resumed full control of his realm – though he had to tread carefully so as not to upset the fragile peace that had been established.

This must have come as a blow for Llywelyn, for in de Montfort's last months in power he had gained the peace treaty and the recognition of his position in Wales that he had long cherished. Fortunately for Llywelyn, Henry did not feel strong enough to take on the Welsh prince and, in an effort to establish peace, he agreed to honour the terms of the agreement previously concluded with de Montfort. Thus, in September 1267, Llywelyn did homage to Henry by a ford on the Severn that marked the frontier between the Welsh and English, and the treaty of Montgomery was signed.

According to the terms of the treaty Henry granted Llywelyn and his successors by hereditary right the principality of Wales and the right to be called Prince of Wales. He was granted the homage of all the Welsh princes and lords of Wales, with the exception of Maredudd ap Rhys Gryg. The price of peace was high. Llywelyn was required to pay 25,000 marks for the treaty; 5000 marks were due immediately or by Christmas, and the remainder in instalments of around 3000 marks a year. According to T. Jones Pierce this treaty was a '*tour de force* of great constitutional significance' that raised Llywelyn to 'a unique place among the great figures of Welsh history as the sponsor of the first experiment in Welsh *statehood*'.

Llywelyn had reached the high point of his career, but the problems did not go away. His brother Dafydd was a constant thorn in his side, as was Gruffudd ap Gwenwynwyn, and when the two of them plotted to have him killed in 1274 he at last determined to act and resolve the conflict between them once and for all.

Unfortunately for Llywelyn both traitors fled to England seeking the protection of the new king Edward I. Edward's decision to give the fugitives refuge in his realm had far-reaching implications in Anglo-Welsh relations. Henceforth, Llywelyn reacted with undisguised contempt and disgust at the king's favoured treatment of the traitors, which may partly explain why he became awkward when homage and payments of the sums agreed at Montgomery were demanded.

Llywelyn was invited to Edward's coronation in August 1274 but did not attend. Nor did he attend the king when summoned to do so at Shrewsbury in 1273, or Chester in 1275, to pay homage. In a letter to Pope Gregory, Llywelyn set out his reasons for not attending the king, saying it was because he felt it was unsafe for him to do so as he would be with the men, Dafydd and Gruffudd, who had plotted his death. In retaliation, Llywelyn decided to fulfil his promise to marry the daughter of Simon de Montfort and in 1275 she sailed from France to wed her suitor. However, her ship was intercepted near the Isles of Scilly and she was taken into Edward's custody.

The matter could only be resolved by war. In the spring of 1277 Edward declared war on Llywelyn. Launching the main offensive against Gwynedd from Chester, the main royal army advanced to Conwy and another force occupied Anglesey. Surrounded and cut off from his food supplies Llywelyn had no choice but to concede defeat. The terms of treaty of Aberconwy, signed in November 1277, were harsh: Llywelyn was allowed to retain the style 'prince of Wales', with the homage of five minor lords, but his broader principality was destroyed. It was a chastened Llywelyn who welcomed the king to Worcester cathedral in 1278 to celebrate his marriage to Eleanor de Montfort.

For the next four years Llywelyn tried to live within the terms of the peace treaty, but tension rose particularly in matters connected with landed disputes. The issue often centered on whether matters in dispute should be decided by Welsh or English law. Edward quite naturally preferred to keep all legal matters under the control of his justices, hence his opposition to the use of Welsh law. Needless to say Llywelyn opposed this. But when the renewal of conflict came it did not come from either Edward I or Llywelyn, but from the latter's brother Dafydd.

Dafydd's attack on Hawarden Castle in March 1282 took Llywelyn by surprise. Unwilling at first to join the war on the English, Llywelyn soon decided he had no choice but to throw in his lot with his brother. If he refrained from the war, and by some miracle Dafydd won significant concessions, then he would likely forfeit his position as Prince of Wales. It is likely that the key factor in prompting Llywelyn to join the war was the scale of the support Dafydd's rebellion had engendered throughout Wales: clearly English domination was not popular.

After initial success the war went badly for the Welsh. Anglesey was lost, along with the Perfeddwlad. In June Llywelyn suffered a hammer blow to his ambitions when his wife Eleanor died giving birth to their daughter Gwenllian. Llywelyn's attempts to negotiate an end to the war by outlining the reasons for his rebellion did not impress Edward I. Even the intervention of Archbishop Pecham, who met Llywelyn at his court at Aber near Bangor, could do little to stop the conflict: Edward, it seems, was determined to destroy Llywelyn once and for all.

Leaving his brother to defend Gwynedd, Llywelyn moved south to open a new front against the encroaching English armies. Although the Welsh foiled an attempt by the English to force a crossing of the Menai Strait there was precious little good news. In fact, matters went from bad to worse when news came through to Dafydd that his brother had been killed in December 1282 near Cilmeri in the lordship of Builth. That he died in a skirmish, rather than in a full-scale battle leading his troops, has caused some historians to suggest that Llywelyn was the victim of a conspiracy.

Certainly, the *Brut y Tywysogyon* states that 'there was effected the betrayal of Llywelyn in the belfry at Bangor by his own men'. The precise meaning of the statement is uncertain, but it may suggest that some of Llywelyn's key advisers (perhaps even his own brother Dafydd) may have been plotting with the English to oust him.

It is believed that Llywelyn was lured to Builth by Edmund

Mortimer and other, unnamed English nobles, who held out the prospect of an alliance. Related to the Mortimers by marriage, Llywelyn may have hoped that some of the English nobility had turned against the Crown as de Montfort had done twenty years before. In the event it proved to be a trap, and after a fierce fight, in which the prince was separated from his forces, he was killed.

Llywelyn was decapitated. His head was sent to Edward in Rhuddlan and displayed to his troops before it was taken to London and, crowned with ivy, placed upon a pole at the Tower. Llywelyn's body is believed to have been taken by monks to be buried in the nearby Cistercian abbey of Cwm-hir. After Llywelyn's death his brother Dafydd ap Gruffudd assumed the princeship of Wales, and continued the struggle until his capture in the summer of 1283.

Llywelyn's death inspired elegies of great eloquence by Bleddyn Fardd and Gruffudd ab yr Ynad Coch but they could not hide the fact that his death, followed by that of his brother, was a disaster for Wales. It is perhaps a measure of his failure that history has been unkind to Llywelyn for it is a fact that today, Owain Glyndŵr, is better remembered and more roundly praised than Llywelyn, 'our last leader'.

Dafydd ap Gruffudd

Dafydd ap Gruffudd (d. 1283), last prince of Gwynedd, was the third of four sons of Gruffudd ap Llywelyn (d. 1244) and his wife, Senana. As a younger son, Dafydd had the unenviable task of coping with the knowledge that he would never succeed to the kingdom. His role was that of compliant ally, a man of princely birth who must do as his brother bade him or lose everything. It was a role that Dafydd was simply not fitted to play, and his dissembling character and duplicitious nature earned for him a place in the rogue's gallery of those scorned by history.

Dafydd first appears in the historical record in August 1241 when he and his younger brother Rhodri were delivered into the custody of Henry III. They were given as a pledge of their mother's good faith in an agreement with the king to secure the release of her husband, Gruffudd, from imprisonment by his half-brother, Dafydd ap Llywelyn (d. 1246). Clearly neither Dafydd nor his younger brother Rhodri were included in the share of the family patrimony that saw Gwynedd divided between his elder brothers Owain and Llywelyn ap Gruffudd.

When Dafydd came of age he was appointed *penteulu* or captain of the household troops of his brother Owain. To be entrusted with this important office is a powerful indication of his elder brother's faith in his fidelity. By 1252 Owain went further and invested Dafydd with his first significant landholding, the commote of Cymydmaen in the lordship of Llŷn.

Dissatisfied with his acquisitions thus far Dafydd pressed his claims upon the king and a year later, in 1253, Henry III promised to support him if he was able to secure for himself a still greater portion of Gwynedd. Following the customary method of divide and rule, Henry III was evidently using Dafydd's ambition to serve his own need to keep the dynasts of Gwynedd weak and at odds with each other.

Unlike Owain, Llywelyn was opposed to his younger brother having any further portion of Gwynedd. Given Llywelyn's determination to restrict his brother's land claims it is no wonder that negotiations sponsored by the king failed to produce any results. In 1255 Dafydd had somehow persuaded Owain to join him in an attack on Llywelyn but they were defeated at Bryn Derwin and imprisoned. For reasons known only to himself Llywelyn released Dafydd after little more than a year but he kept Owain imprisoned in the castle of Dolbadarn for the next twenty-two years.

In fact, Llywelyn went further, for having dispossessed Owain he now invested Dafydd with a substantial landholding known as the Perfeddwlad. Captured from the Crown in 1256 Llywelyn hoped to detach his brother from his alliance with Henry III by giving him property once held by the king. In this way, Dafydd not only had to defend his new landholding from his erstwhile ally, but his interests now coincided with those of his brother. It was a clever piece of politicking and is evidence of Llywelyn's astute judgement, but it also reveals the shallowness of Dafydd's character.

For the next seven years Dafydd served his brother loyally: in 1258 he participated in a campaign in south-west Wales and appeared alongside Llywelyn in a record of an agreement between the princes of Wales and a group of Scottish magnates. In 1260 Dafydd was sufficiently trusted by his brother to be given the task of negotiating an end to the 'cold war' that had developed between Llywelyn and Henry III. Henry's distrust, even hatred, of his former ally had developed to such a pitch that when, in the summer of 1262, the king heard a rumour that Llywelyn had died he determined that Dafydd should not succeed his brother to the supremacy that the latter had established in Wales.

Where Henry III had failed in binding Dafydd to a servile clientship his son and heir Prince Edward thought he might succeed. In early 1263, Prince Edward may have detected friction in the relationship between Dafydd and Llywelyn for he entered into secret negotiations with him. The result of their parley was Edward's commitment to support Dafydd should he decide to challenge his brother's supremacy and seize from him what he believed to be his rightful landed inheritance in Gwynedd. In serving to fuel Dafydd's ambition Edward hoped to divide the brothers and thereby encourage a civil war in Wales. Ironically, when civil war did broke out it did so not in Wales, but in England!

The prospect of being his own man, supported by the Crown with landholdings to match his status as a prince, inevitably led to Dafydd's defection. If Dafydd had hoped to ignite a rebellion against his brother he was sadly mistaken. Even a military expedition to Wales led by Edward and supported by Dafydd failed to dent Llywelyn's power and authority in the principality; it remained intact and suffered no diminution. Though doubtless angered by his brother's betrayal, Llywelyn did nothing to further provoke the English. It may have seemed to Dafydd that he had backed the wrong side, for less than eighteen months after deserting his brother for pastures new, his new-found ally was himself in difficulty and facing the prospect of losing his power.

In 1264 the Crown found itself besieged by a breakaway group of rebellious barons under the command of Simon de Montfort. De Montfort wished to reform what he believed was a corrupt and failed government under Henry III. While Llywelyn greeted with glee the news that civil war had broken out in England, Dafydd watched in despair. Llywelyn sided with de Montfort, who scored a notable success in capturing the king and his son Prince Edward, while Dafydd remained aloof from proceedings. In fact, Dafydd found time to get married: he wed Elizabeth Ferrers, sister of the earl of Derby, and widow of William Marshal. Through his wife Dafydd became a landholder in England taking possession of her manor of Folesham in Norfolk (which he later exchanged with John Marshal for the manor of Norton, Northamptonshire).

It was left to Prince Edward to escape captivity, rescue his father and then defeat de Montfort and his rebel army at Evesham in 1265. The fact that Llywelyn had supplied de Montfort with a sizeable contingent of Welsh foot soldiers did little to alter the outcome of the battle. With de Monfort's death the civil war came quickly to an end. Henry III was restored, but he had to tread carefully for fear of upsetting the delicate truce that had been established in England.

Taking advantage of the king's weakness Llywelyn bargained hard for a change in their relationship, and the Crown of England was brought to a position where it had no choice but to formally recognize Llywelyn as Prince of Wales. One can only wonder at how Dafydd greeted the news of his brother's triumph in signing the treaty of Montgomery in 1267. It was, presumably, a chastened Dafydd who accepted his brother's magnanimous offer to forget his betrayal and restore him to his former position of influence within the Welsh political establishment. However, their reconciliation became stuck on the issue of landholding when Llywelyn made clear his intention to restore to his brother only those territories he had held prior to his defection in 1263.

Dafydd was bitterly disappointed. His resentment boiled beneath the surface, but outwardly he behaved as the dutiful younger brother of the ruling prince. Thus it was that when Llywelyn led a military expedition to Glamorgan in 1271 Dafydd is to be found among his senior captains. By 1274 Dafydd could no longer contain his anger, and in that year he and Gruffudd ap Gwenwynwyn of Southern Powys conspired to kill Llywelyn.

Alerted to the plot, Llywelyn summoned his brother's confederate Gruffudd to appear before the ruling council. There Gruffudd and his son Owain were convicted of infidelity and the latter was taken into custody as a pledge of his father's good conduct. Why Llywelyn did not summon or proceed against his brother is not known, but Dafydd was living on borrowed time.

A few months later the young Owain ap Gruffudd ap Gwenwynwyn confessed all to Llywelyn who then summoned Dafydd to appear before him and his council at Rhuddlan to answer charges of treason. Dafydd failed to appear but was given a second chance to turn up at his brother's court at Llanfor in Penllyn. Again Dafydd failed to appear, but this time he fled to England with an armed following. He was joined by Gruffudd ap Gwenwynwyn, who left his son Owain to face Llywelyn's wrath alone.

Having succeeded his father in 1272 King Edward I welcomed both Dafydd and Gruffudd to his court where they were housed and suitably entertained. This time there would be no reconciliation between Llywelyn and his brother. Indeed, Llywelyn was so angered by the king's courteous treatment of a man he considered to be a traitor that he refused to meet and do homage to Edward at Chester in 1275. Llywelyn demanded of the king that he return the two who had conspired to kill him. Edward I declined, but used the opportunity afforded by Llywelyn's refusal to do homage, a clear breach of the terms of the treaty of Montgomery, to declare war on his obstinate vassal.

In the war of 1277 Dafydd served in the king's forces alongside William Beauchamp, earl of Warwick. Based at Chester the invading Anglo-Welsh army advanced into Powys Fadog where it encountered little opposition. In fact, Llywelyn's forces were ill-prepared for a long drawn-out campaign and within months of the outbreak of war he capitulated. Dafydd must have waited with some anticipation as to what his reward would be. At the very least he hoped to secure a half share of Gwynedd but the king made plain his desire to include the long incarcerated Owain in his plan for the division of Gwynedd.

Divided between three brothers, Llywelyn, Owain and Dafydd (the youngest, Rhodri, was apparently excluded, being given a cash settlement instead), the portions of land allotted to each were likely to satisfy none but Owain. The terms of the peace treaty of Aberconwy must have come as a blow to Dafydd, for while Llywelyn was granted a life-interest in Gwynedd Uwch Conwy, and the retention of his title as Prince of Wales, all Dafydd got was an 'acknowledgement' of his hereditary right there. The vagueness of this agreement was hardly likely to satisfy Dafydd, but worse was to follow when he learnt that the king had decided that his reward was to be granted only a life-interest in the lordships of Dyffryn Clwyd and Rhufoniog.

Clearly irritated by Edward's failure to reward him properly, Dafydd soon began to complain about other matters regarding the overdue payment of his troops and his right to keep the booty taken by them in Powys. Nevertheless, although resentful of his treatment by Edward I, Dafydd opted to play the dutiful vassal, a role he was used to by this stage, and accept the situation. Whether or not Edward trusted Dafydd is unknown, but in an effort to soothe his obvious disappointment the king offered to help him build a castle at Caergwrle. As a further gesture of goodwill the king bestowed on Dafydd the manor of Frodsham in Cheshire: this too was only for life.

Dafydd's patience lasted a further three years until 1281, when he became involved in a dispute over the ownership of lands in the lordship of Hope, close to where he was building his castle of Caergwrle. Summoned to appear in the county court of Chester to answer the claim submitted by William de Venables, Dafydd protested that the case should be heard according to Welsh rather than English law. In fact, according to Llywelyn's biographer, the distinguished historian, J. Beverley Smith, Dafydd:

> in a loud voice, declared that the land was in Wales and that he had no need to answer in the county court. He pleaded that the laws of Wales be respected like the laws of other nations.

Unwilling to make further appearances in court, let alone recognise the authority of English law, Dafydd resorted to war to bring the case to an end. In March 1282 Dafydd launched an attack on the castles of Rhuddlan and Hawarden, though he was only successful in capturing the latter along with its English constable Roger Clifford.

Certainly inspired, if not actively encouraged, by Dafydd's resort to arms, some of the other Welsh princes, too, rose in rebellion and attacked English castles elsewhere in Wales. After initial hesitation Llywelyn also rebelled and threw in his lot with his brother. The second, and last, War of Welsh Independence had begun.

The fighting was fierce but the English gradually wore down the Welsh. As Llywelyn left to open another front in mid-Wales he left Dafydd to defend Gwynedd. When news came that his brother had been killed near Builth in December 1282, Dafydd assumed the role and title of Prince of Wales. Having achieved his life's ambition

Dafydd now found himself in a fight for survival. His Princeship of Wales lasted little more than seven months when, in June 1283, he was betrayed by his own men and delivered to Edward I. He was imprisoned at Rhuddlan and, three months later, was brought to Shrewsbury to stand trial. According to J. Beverley Smith:

> Edward expressed his anger at the perfidy of one whom the king had received as an exile, nourished as an orphan, and endowed with lands and placed among the great ones at court.

Dafydd was tried and sentenced to death for treason. He was dragged to the scaffold and hanged, after which he was cut down, disembowelled and his entrails burnt. Dafydd's head was placed beside that of his brother above traitor's gate at the Tower of London. Following their capture, Dafydd's sons, Llywelyn and Owain, were taken prisoners to Bristol Castle. Llywelyn died and was buried there in 1287, whilst Owain endured nearly forty years of incarceration before he too succumbed to death.

Rhodri alone of the four brothers survived the war (Owain had died some time before) and because he took no part in the conflict he was given a pension with an estate in England, where he remained for the rest of his life. His grandson Owain ap Thomas ap Rhodri, better known as Owain Lawgoch, briefly fanned the flames of Welsh independence some ninety years later before he, too, was betrayed and murdered by an assassin in 1378.

Gwenllian, daughter and heiress of Llywelyn ap Gruffudd

Given that the history of Medieval Wales, with few exceptions, has been written about by men, it is perhaps not surprising that precious little is known about Llywelyn's heir Gwenllian. Born in June 1282, she never knew her mother, who died giving birth to her, or her father, from whom she was taken when only six months old. In a world dominated by men it would have been highly unlikely that Gwenllian would have received the kind of support that was necessary for her to assume the leadership of Wales. With the death of her father the title of Prince of Wales passed to Dafydd and from him, given the opportunity, to his sons, Llywelyn and Owain.

Nevertheless, although Gwenllian would have been bypassed in the struggle for political and military authority she did possess one priceless attribute: her royal identity. As the daughter of Llywelyn her hand in marriage would have been highly prized by those willing to seize the opportunity to exploit her lineage and familial heritage. This perhaps explains why the baby Gwenllian – she was aged no more than seventeen months –was removed to the Gilbertine nunnery at Sempringham in Lincolnshire. When she was older and at an age to make her own decisions she was, according to the Welsh chronicles, made to take her vows against her will and become a nun. It is reported that Edward I justified his action thus:

> having the Lord before our eyes, pitying also her sex and age, that the innocent and unwitting may not seem to atone for the iniquity and ill-doing of the wicked and contemplating specially the life of your Order.

In 1288, some four years after Gwenllian was admitted to Sempringham, Edward instructed Thomas Normanvill:

> to go to the places where the daughters of Llewellyn and of David his brother, who have taken the veil in the Order of

Sempringham, are dwelling, and to report upon their state and custody by the next Parliament.

It is known that Dafydd's daughters, one of whom was named Gwladus (d. 1328) were sent to the Gilbertine house of Sixle, Lincolnshire, and other nunneries. Like Gwenllian they too endured virtual imprisonment within the walls of an English convent.

The confined walls of the monastery or nunnery had long been used to incarcerate females who represented a possible threat to the state. Unlike common women, noble or royal females were shut up to prevent them being used as political pawns whereby they might be forced into marriage and having children. In rare cases like Gwenllian they were confined when very young so that they were brought up and educated in a nunnery. By the time they were teenagers or young women the monastic life was all they had ever known and so they were unlikely to challenge the authority of the monastic rule or question their life of confinement.

We hear of Gwenllian only once more before her death in 1337. In 1327 Edward I's grandson, Edward III, stayed at Sempringham where he met Gwenllian, granting her a generous yearly pension of £20 for life. Thereafter she fades into obscurity, to be rescued six hundred years later by the Princess Gwenllian Society, which erected a memorial in 1993 as a tribute to the princess.

Owain Glyndŵr

It is argued that the Age of the Princes in Wales ended officially in December 1282 with the killing of Llywelyn ap Gruffudd by the forces of Edward I, King of England. One poet composed the 'Llywelyn Ein Llyw Olaf' ('Llywelyn Our Last Leader') line of *cynghanedd* in memory of him and that stayed in common parlance as a royal nickname for him. Few mourned the death of his brother Dafydd who continued the fight until his capture and execution by Edward I in October 1283. Thus Llywelyn may indeed be regarded as the last leader of the old princely order.

Edward I sought to make his victory complete by building castles to subdue the Welsh and by defending the new boroughs he established within secure walls. He aimed to colonize Wales by inducing English migrants to settle in the country for which the native populace were expected to make way to accommodate these new landowners. Some have referred to this as a medieval example of ethnic cleansing and have cited examples to support their contention. One such example is recorded in a document noting that knights returning from a campaign of clearing the surrounding lands of rebels were paid a shilling for every head they brought back to Flint castle.

The subjugation of the Welsh was seemingly completed in 1284 with the imposition of the Statute of Rhuddlan which reduced the Welsh people to a servile position in the new order.

However, the urge of the Welsh to be free of the oppressive rule by castle and their unwillingness to yield to the new governance led to a number of uprisings. However, rebellions by Madog ap Llewelyn, descended from the princes of Gwynedd, in 1293–4 and by Llywelyn Bren in Morgannwg in 1317–18 failed. Undaunted by these setbacks the Welsh poets prophecied that a warrior, the fabled 'Son of Destiny', would one day come to rescue his people and rid the nation of its English oppressors. 'Owain' is one of the fabled names for the Son of Destiny in Welsh legends. A man of that name – Owain Lawgoch – emerged in the 1360s ready to fulfil the prophecy. As the grandson of Rhodri, Llywelyn the Last's brother, his princely credentials were impeccable. He fought as a captain of Welsh soldiers in the service of the King of France against the English. However, his plans to invade Wales with a Franco-Welsh army were thwarted when he was murdered by an assassin hired by the English Crown.

Twenty years were to elapse before a Welshman would again challenge the power of the English crown. This man too would be hailed as the mythical 'Son of Destiny' but unlike those before him his name, fame and reputation has endured. That man was Owain Glyndŵr.

Owain ap Gruffudd Fychan was born, either at Carrog or Sycharth, sometime between 1354 and 1359 (the latter date being the more probable). Through his father, Gruffudd Fychan he was directly descended from the Princes of Powys Fadog. Indeed, had the conquest of Wales by Edward I not been so complete he might have expected to one day rule the kingdom of his ancestors but this was not to be. As it was he had to content himself with what remained of his family's once considerable patrimony namely, the minor lordship of Glyndyfrdwy (from where he took his name) and a part share of the lordship of Cynllaith. His great-great grandfather Gruffudd Fychan ap Gruffudd ap Madog was one of the few princely survivors of the conquest of 1282–3, and by the early fourteenth century Gruffudd's son, Madog, was holding Glyndyfrdwy and Cynllaith of the king in chief by Welsh barony, a landed estate that provided a not inconsiderable annual income of some 300 marks. His chief residence at Sycharth in Cynllaith was described by the poet Iolo Goch as a modern, half-timbered, tiled, and chimneyed house, set on a motte, with chapel, bakehouse and mill.

Through his mother, Elen, daughter of Owain ap Thomas ap Llywelyn, Owain could claim descent from the stock of the Lord Rhys, princes of Deheubarth. In territorial terms this amounted to part possession of the half-commotes of Iscoed Uwch Hirwen and Gwynionydd Is Cerdyn in Cardiganshire, and perhaps a share of the manor of Trefgarn in Pembrokeshire.

Apart from being descended of impeccable Welsh princely stock, a fact noted by Iolo Goch, we know precious little about Glyndŵr's early life. It is thought he succeeded to his father's estates sometime between 1369–71, when his mother is described as the late wife of 'Gruffudd of Glyndyfrdwy'. If this is the case then Glyndŵr succeeded as a minor but it is not known who took responsibility for his upbringing and education. It is possible but not certain that the Fitzalan, earls of Arundel, may have had a hand in caring for the young Owain. Documentary evidence points to the family's close associations with the Fitzalans, who were also Marcher lords in Wales by dint of their territorial landholdings at Bromfield and Yale, Oswestry and Chirk. Certainly Glyndŵr benefited from the patronage of powerful men influential enough to secure for him a legal education, perhaps even a place at the Inns of Court, London, having been trained as an apprentice-at-law.

As was typical of a young man of gentle birth, Glyndŵr trained as a soldier which he put to good use in 1384 when he, alongside his brother, Tudur, served under Sir Gregory Sais at Berwick on the Scottish border and under Richard Fitzalan at the blockade of Sluys in 1387. Glyndŵr mixed freely with men of gentle birth, both Welsh and English, a fact that enabled him to secure the hand of Margaret Hanmer, whose father, Sir David, served the Fitzalan earls of Arundel as a member of their marcher council in 1386–7. Glyndŵr and his brother Tudur are named among the esquires of the retinue of Richard Fitzalan mustered on 13 March 1387, and Glyndŵr's name headed the list of Arundel's esquires mustered for overseas service in May 1388. Clearly, Glyndŵr moved among the Welsh and Marcher elite with ease, a fact noted in 1386 when he gave evidence, along with Tudur, his brother, and John Hanmer and Robert Puleston, his brothers-in-law, to a court of chivalry held at Chester.

Unfortunately for Glyndŵr, his family and friends, political events in England were to take an unexpected turn for the worse when, in 1399, Richard II was deposed by Henry, duke of Lancaster, who assumed the title of King Henry IV. It soon became clear that men like Glyndŵr, who had done well under the old regime, would be treated with suspicion until their loyalty could be proven. Glyndŵr was never given that chance.

Contemporary evidence for the causes of Glyndŵr's uprising is rather thin on the ground, but according to two English chronicles, namely, the *Annales Henrici quarti*, of St Albans and the *Vita Ricardi secundi* of Evesham, the rebellion was caused by a territorial dispute between the lord of Dyffryn Clwyd, Reynold Grey, and his neighbour Glyndŵr. To add fuel to the fire, Grey is also thought to have blackened Glyndŵr's reputation by withholding a summons to appear before the new king which was taken as a sign of disloyalty.

According to the sworn testimony of a Shropshire jury, taken on 25 October 1400, Glyndŵr, together with his brother Tudur, his son Gruffudd, his Hanmer and Puleston brothers-in-law, Hywel Cyffin, dean of St Asaph, and Crach Ffinant, described as 'their prophet', and many other Welshmen, had gathered at Glyndyfrdwy on 16 September to plot rebellion. There they declared Owain to be the rightful prince of Wales and called on Welshmen from across Wales to support their mission to reject Henry IV as their king and to eject the English from their country. Some 270 men heeded his call and they joined Glyndŵr on an attack of the 'English towns' of Ruthin, Denbigh, Rhuddlan, Flint, Hawarden, Holt, Oswestry, and Welshpool.

On hearing of the Welsh uprising Henry IV made his way towards Shrewsbury, but after a show of force the king was content to leave north Wales in early October certain the insurrection had been quelled. Soon offers of pardon were made to rebels across north Wales excepting Glyndŵr and his Anglesey cousins Rhys and Gwilym ap Tudur who had also risen in rebellion. Glyndŵr's lands in north and south Wales were declared forfeit to the Crown in November 1400, together with those of his cousins. Whereas Glyndŵr lay low during this period his Anglesey cousins took matters into their own hands when, on Good Friday (1 April) 1401, they seized the castle of Conwy: the garrison was at prayer in the church! The castle was not given up by the Welsh, and then only on agreement, until the end of June at which point Glyndŵr's cousins returned home to Anglesey protected by their newly-issued royal pardons.

Unlike his cousins Glyndŵr fared less well suffering a heavy defeat at the hands of John Charlton, lord of Powys. Undeterred Glyndŵr pressed on and in May scored a notable success when he defeated a large force of royal troops drawn mainly form Pembrokeshire. The victory at Hyddgen inspired a wave of support with adherents coming from as far afield as Oxford and Cambridge where a number of Welsh scholars were reported to have thrown down their books in order to take up the implements of war. Welsh labourers working in England returned home to join their locally-based comrades in supporting Glyndŵr. However for the rebellion to succeed Glyndŵr knew that he needed the support of men like himself, gentry with wealth, connections and experience of war. In a letter addressed to Henry Dwn, a leading landowner, soldier, and administrator of the lordship of Cydweli, Glyndŵr called on him to join in the movement to liberate the Welsh from English oppression.

Styling himself Owain ap Gruffudd, lord of Glyndyfrdwy, Glyndŵr had yet to publicly express his ambition, that of becoming the ruling prince of an independent Wales. For this to become a reality Glyndŵr would need to gain further significant successes. Over the next two years the rebellion gathered momentum with lengthy sieges of royal castles such as at Caernarfon adding to the increasing paralysis of royal administration in Wales. Soon the rebels were scoring significant victories in battle over their English opponents. Among the most stunning successes involved the capture of Glyndŵr's nemesis, Reynold Grey in April 1402 followed by the victory in battle over Sir Edmund Mortimer at Pilleth in June. Within weeks of his capture in battle Mortimer had abandoned the Crown and thrown in his lot with Glyndŵr. To cement the alliance Mortimer married Catherine, Glyndŵr's daughter. Grey, on the other hand, was held to ransom and was only released on payment of the considerable sum of 10,000 marks or just over £660.

In spite of a succession of well-armed royal expeditions to Wales in 1401, 1402 and 1403, the Crown failed to catch sight of Glyndŵr let alone meet him in battle where it hoped to defeat and destroy him. Buoyed by his successes Glyndŵr began to seek external alliances, addressing letters in French to the king of Scotland and in Latin to the Gaelic lords of Ireland. Frustrated by its lack of success in putting down the rebellious Welsh, the English government turned instead to enacting a series of Parliamentary statutes designed to restrict and punish their Cymric neighbours.

According to the terms of the penal statutes the Welsh were prohibited from holding public assemblies (a gathering of more than three Welshmen was considered a threat!), the bearing of arms, the importation of victuals or armour, the keeping of castles or the holding of office. Even Englishmen married to Welshwomen were not spared the penalty of the law being denied office in Wales and the possible forfeiture of their landed property. In fact, anyone suspected of aiding or perhaps even sympathising with 'Owen ap Glendourdy, traitor to our sovereign lord and king' was threatened with prosecution. The harsh penal statutes did little to halt Glyndŵr's progress or dent his growing reputation. The English had to be content with minor and somewhat meaningless successes such as that in May 1403 when Prince Henry (Shakespeare's Prince Hal and the future victor at Agincourt), as royal lieutenant in Wales, burned Glyndŵr's house at Sycharth and ravaged his estate in Glyndyfrdwy.

The years between the summer of 1403 and spring of 1406 are generally regarded as the high-water mark of the Glyndŵr rebellion. A successful expedition to Carmarthenshire in the summer of 1403 netted him further support as well as the capture of the castles of Carreg Cennen, Dryslwyn, Newcastle Emlyn, and, most notably, Carmarthen, the centre of royal government and administration in south-west Wales. Backed by a reported army of over 8000 men Glyndŵr's star was very much in the ascendant. Cracks soon appeared in the Crown's support when one of the kingdom's leading baronial families, the Percies of Northumberland, rose in rebellion.

Although allied with Glyndŵr, the leaders of the rebellion, Henry 'Hotspur' Percy, heir to the earldom and his uncle Thomas, earl of Worcester, chose to go it alone when they met the king in battle near

Shrewsbury. Their defeat and death in battle in July 1403 was a blow to Glyndŵr but it did little to check his continuing success in Wales. Indeed, the appearance that autumn of French and Breton ships in Welsh waters actively aiding Glyndŵr's forces in besieging the castles of Cydweli and Caernarfon not only signalled the intervention of hostile foreign powers in the rebellion but also augured the conclusion of a treaty of alliance between the aspirant Welsh prince and the French king, Charles VI.

The capture of Aberystwyth and Harlech castles by rebel forces during 1404 confirmed Glyndŵr's growing power. In fact, so sure was he of his position in Wales that he now publicly claimed to be the rightful ruler of the Principality. Thus, in July 1404 did the French king negotiate and conclude a treaty of alliance 'in the fourth year of his principate' with 'the magnificent and mighty Owen, Prince of Wales'. Both parties promised that neither would enter into a separate peace with Henry IV and although no formal promise of military assistance was given or received the French were provided with a list of key ports and seaways.

Holding his court at Harlech castle, Glyndŵr soon acquired the trappings of statehood as may be witnessed by contemporary references to letters patent, to a council, chancellor, secretary, notaries, and proctors, and to the prince's privy and great seals. In short, here was a prince of an emerging state who could call on the services of a trained and experienced bureaucracy. This was followed by his calling of parliaments at Machynlleth and Harlech respectively, the drawing up of plans for an independent Welsh Church with the archbishopric of St. David's at its head, and the setting up of two universities; one in the north and the other in the south.

So confident of success had he become, at least outwardly, that he negotiated the so-called tripartite agreement between himself, Edmund Mortimer and Henry Percy, earl of Northumberland. This agreed the division of England and Wales, with Glyndŵr taking as his share a greatly extended Wales that stretched to the river Severn and to the source of the Trent and Mersey. Unfortunately for Glyndŵr, this agreement never became a reality for Northumberland failed to revenge himself on Henry IV for the death of his heir Hotspur when his rebellion, too, ended in disaster.

Undaunted Glyndŵr pressed on and he was rewarded for his endeavours when, in the summer of 1405, the French dispatched troops to Wales. Landing at Milford Haven early in August 1405, the French force of 2500 men was soon joined at the siege of Haverfordwest by Glyndŵr leading a reported 10,000 strong army. Although the castle held out the town fell to Glyndŵr and his French allies along with the towns and castles of Cardigan and Carmarthen. Moving east the Franco-Welsh army reached Worcester where it halted for a week but failed to engage the English army under King Henry. If militarily the expedition failed to achieve anything of note, economically the Welsh struck a notable victory with the seizure of the king's baggage train, loaded with provisions and jewels.

Unbeknown to Glyndŵr this expedition to England was to be the high point of his rebellion. Defeats soon followed and at the battle of Pwll Melyn near Usk, Glyndwr lost his son, Gruffudd, to capture, and his brother, Tudur, who was killed. By the end of 1406 the people of the Gower, Carmarthenshire, Ceredigion, and Anglesey had largely deserted Glyndŵr.

Within months of the submission of the people of Ceredigion the castle of Aberystwyth was closely besieged by troops led by Prince Henry, it fell to the English by the end of 1408. Two to three months later, in February 1409, Harlech too had fallen to English troops after a prolonged siege in which Edmund Mortimer died. Although Glyndŵr managed to make his escape his family, including his wife, two of his daughters, and his granddaughters lodged in the castle had been taken prisoner and sent to London. The rebellion lingered on for a further six years but as each year passed the Welsh grew weaker while the English grew stronger.

The last great raid led by Glyndŵr on the Shropshire border took place in 1412, after which no more is heard of him. It is thought that he died sometime in 1415. He was almost certainly dead by April 1417, when the Crown offered his son Maredudd a pardon if he would give himself up. In spite of many offers of pardon Glyndŵr refused to surrender and he died in hiding, quite possibly in what is today Herefordshire. There is a strong tradition linking him to Kentchurch, the home of the Scudamore family whose head, Sir John, had married Glyndŵr's daughter Alice. The last words of one of the chronicles of the story of Glyndŵr tell: 'Some say he died; the poets say he did not.' The poets saw the sense in keeping alive the myth that the last prince had never left the land. Considering how much the poets valued him it is surprising to discover they never composed an elegy in his honour. But that in itself is significant. It would have been like placing a tombstone on the Age of the Princes – the age when Wales was governed by the Welsh.

Down the centuries, the legend that is Owain Glyndŵr has grown to become an iconic symbol of Welsh pride and independence. He is lauded as a national hero and is regarded by many as a Welshman of exceptional ability possessed of statesmanlike vision and imagination. Rather than embodying a bridge back to the Age of the Princes, he has come to be regarded as a bridge forward to the Wales of the future. By the end of the twentieth century some of the main aims he set for himself and his rebellion in the Pennal Letter had been realized. The University of Wales was established in 1872; the Church of Wales, independent of the state Church of England, was established in 1920; the Welsh-language was re-established as an official language of law courts, council chambers and local government, and in 1997 self-governance came back to Wales. Now, in the twenty-first century, the most charismatic and the most heroic of the princes is regarded not as one of the last leaders of a golden age, but as the first leader of a modern Wales.